Citizenship

This book outlines a critical theory of citizenship, with an emphasis on how citizenship institutes power relations and organises the rights and obligations of those who become its subjects.

Whether it is the question of the rights of animals, children, migrants, minorities, mothers, or mountains, and whether such rights are protected or guaranteed by national law, international law, or human rights law, the issue of citizenship has already indelibly marked the 21st century. As an institution, citizenship governs the relationship between a polity and its peoples by dividing them into citizens and noncitizens, with differentiated rights and obligations. So necessarily, this book argues, citizenship is an institution of domination and emancipation that brings into play the struggles of those who want to protect certain privileges and the struggles of those who are against being caught in either second-class or noncitizen categories. Deconstructing dominant theories and practices of citizenship, a critical theory of citizenship must, therefore, not only analyse intersecting rights, but also connect citizenship to these broader social struggles. For it is these struggles, the book maintains, that give meaning to citizenship itself.

The book will be of interest to scholars and students in sociolegal studies, sociology, politics, and as well as those working in citizenship, migration, and refugee studies.

Engin Isin is Professor Emeritus of International Politics at Queen Mary University of London.

New Trajectories in Law

series editors
Adam Gearey, Birkbeck College, University of London
Prabha Kotiswaran, Kings College London
Colin Perrin, Commissioning Editor, Routledge
Mariana Valverde, University of Toronto

for information about the series and details of previous and forthcoming titles, see https://www.routledge.com/New-Trajectories-in-Law/book-series/NTL

A GlassHouse Book

Citizenship

New Trajectories in Law

Engin Isin

Routledge
Taylor & Francis Group

a GlassHouse book

First published 2024
by Routledge
4 Park Square, Milton Park, Abingdon, Oxon OX14 4RN

and by Routledge
605 Third Avenue, New York, NY 10158

Routledge is an imprint of the Taylor & Francis Group, an informa business

a GlassHouse book

British Library Cataloguing-in-Publication Data
A catalogue record for this book is available from the British Library

Library of Congress Cataloging-in-Publication Data
Names: Isin, Engin F. (Engin Fahri), 1959- author.
Title: Citizenship : new trajectories in law / Engin Isin.
Description: Abingdon, Oxon [UK] ; New York,
NY : Routledge, 2024. |
Series: New trajectories in law | Includes bibliographical
references and index.
Identifiers: LCCN 2024001270 (print) | LCCN 2024001271 (ebook) |
ISBN 9781032497648 (hardback) | ISBN 9781032499000 (paperback) |
ISBN 9781003395997 (ebook)
Subjects: LCSH: Citizenship.
Classification: LCC K3224 .I85 2024 (print) | LCC K3224 (ebook) |
DDC 342.08/3--dc23/eng/20240117
LC record available at https://lccn.loc.gov/2024001270
LC ebook record available at https://lccn.loc.gov/2024001271

ISBN: 978-1-032-49764-8 (hbk)
ISBN: 978-1-032-49900-0 (pbk)
ISBN: 978-1-003-39599-7 (ebk)

DOI: 10.4324/9781003395997

Typeset in Sabon
by Taylor & Francis Books

Contents

Tables

Preface

This book articulates a concept of citizenship. The multiple uses of citizenship are overlapping – and conflicting. Each embodies different and sometimes opposite lineages, trajectories, and inheritances. A particular lineage understands citizenship as a critical attitude or orientation toward the present by placing us within historical series at least in the last 2,500 years (when citizenship was named as such), if not 6,000 years (when subjects of politics emerged). This perspective draws from a deep history of the origins of ancient polities and the development (or not) of political subjectivities in subsequent polities such as cities, states, companies, empires, leagues, and federations. The purpose of articulating a concept, as Gilles Deleuze says, 'is not a matter of bringing all sorts of things together under one concept but rather of relating each concept to variables that explain its mutations' ([1980] 1995, 31). A concept such as citizenship inevitably involves other concepts such as noncitizenship, strangers, outsiders, foreigners, aliens, peoples, the people, and many more in different sites and senses of use. Our objective here is not to provide a coherent or stable concept of citizenship but to understand how citizenship functions and its transformations.

A concept is always performative as it is a revaluation, citation, repetition, reiteration, resignification, and transformation of heterogenous uses for identifying and tackling problems. A speech act, as an utterance, can neither be merely descriptive nor just explanatory. It is performative: it brings into being that which it claims to describe or explain. A concept of citizenship we articulate in this book arises from and combines two uses of citizenship.

Citizenship enables people to develop their sense of being political subjects for making rights claims of, in, or by accepting (or rejecting) obligations. This use of citizenship signifies it as an institution of emancipation because it presupposes autonomous subjects (free to act). We are familiar with the much-repeated utterance 'from subjects to citizens'.

We complicate this use of citizenship by staging it with another use, which involves domination because it presupposes dependent subjects (unfree to act). This second use as domination does not have a recognisable slogan ('from citizens to subjects' would be an appropriate one) but the oppressive and repressive uses of citizenship for impeding people's sense of being political subjects have been well documented. The prominent understanding of *citizenship as emancipation* is so deeply entrenched or, conversely, *citizenship as domination* is rendered invisible so effectively, that it becomes imperative to untangle these two meanings of citizenship. Yet, we will tangle them again to propose *citizenship as an apparatus of government* as a concept that embodies both domination and emancipation.

A couple of moves made writing this book a challenge. The first is to insist on citing, repeating, and reiterating the phrase *citizenship as an apparatus of government* throughout the book to distinguish it from the conventional uses of citizenship. This was necessary to defamiliarise ourselves in every step of the way from the conventional uses of citizenship as its performative utterances appear in our mind's eye as a stable concept: citizenship is membership, citizenship is about rights, citizenship is about duties, citizenship is status, citizenship is practice and so on. To deconstruct a concept to articulate a different one from its ruins is no mean task, and to write it effectively is even harder.

The second move is an attempt to avoid naming historical and geographical events in familiar terms when articulating the concept of citizenship as an apparatus of government. To decolonise signifying events, we borrow a convention from deep history and eschew a religious calendar except when an event is known by its conventional date. So rather than using BC/AD or BCE/CE we shall use 'years ago' convention to indicate in a relational way that we are placing ourselves within historical series from where we stand in the present. This does not always work smoothly or precisely, but it is an attempt to decolonise historical events through which we think politically about citizenship. To decolonise naming places, we also disavow (as much as possible) continents or countries as names that contain events.

These conceptual, historical and geographic decolonising and deconstructing moves may have estranging effects on readers but hopefully they also sharpen some political problems concerning writing about citizenship and indicate ways to address them. As we shall argue next, if we accept that the politics of citizenship is simultaneously the politics of the language of citizenship these moves are necessary to articulate a concept of *citizenship as an apparatus of government*.

We are indebted to numerous and inspiring works produced by activists, artists, scholars, and scientists of which we could only acknowledge a tiny fraction. Those who may read this book will hopefully recognise their immense contribution and our gratefulness.

Introduction

Citizenship as an apparatus of government

The study of ordinary language as the language of politics has revolutionised the politics of language itself. By widening its focus from claims of representation to doing things with words, ordinary language philosophy has challenged social sciences and humanities. How the ordinary language of politics institutes and sustains domination over the dispossessed, marginalised, and subaltern peoples and how peoples overturn dominant descriptions, categories, and classifications became primary struggles of our times. We have experienced a similar movement on the language of citizenship. The ordinary languages of class, race, gender, ability, and others challenged conventional languages of civil, political, and social citizenship by revealing their domination, resignifying their meanings, transforming their functions, and rearticulating diverse ways of becoming citizen subjects. We have seen scholars challenging the dominant languages of citizenship by interpreting ordinary languages of citizenship as political (Fortier 2022; Shindo 2022). We are now at a juncture when citizenship as domination *again* finds its reverse in citizenship as emancipation through ordinary language.

The study of ordinary language as 'ordinary language philosophy' or 'linguistic phenomenology' inaugurated by Ludwig Wittgenstein ([1953] 2009) and J.L. Austin (1962; 1970), where a speech act is understood not only in its meaning but also in its force or use, proved most provocative for studying politics and how ordinary language of politics functions in economic, social, and cultural struggles. The languages of race, gender, class, ability, identity, and belonging have been shown to have not only symbolic but also material effects of domination, and politicising them has been a means of emancipation. The challenge against the ordinary uses of language has been revolutionary.

It was Jacques Derrida who most provocatively deployed and transformed ordinary language philosophy and the meaning and function of performativity ([1977] 1988; [1967] 1978; see Derrida in Sprinker 1999,

DOI: 10.4324/9781003395997-1

224). And Stanley Cavell has shown how language functions in specific situations meaning and intent ([1979] 1999; [1969] 1976). The revolutionary challenge of ordinary language philosophy or linguistic phenomenology is deceptively straightforward (Beaney 2012). When we use language, we are not only describing things, but we are making things, people, and indeed ourselves. Using language involves inhabiting and embodying it when doing things with words. Speech acts are not merely about uttering words: of, in, and by acting through diverse genres of speech (words, images, sounds, gestures, actions) we make ourselves and others with discursive and nondiscursive effects. When we are performing speech acts, we are not merely describing things but are also producing things – we are making ourselves and others happen. Consequently, ordinary language is not only a means of communication, but it is also means of production of peoples and things.

What is meant by ordinary language, for whom it is ordinary, whose usage is ordinary, and who authorises its uses and functions have become political questions (Moati 2014). We have seen scholars studying how people inhabit and embody language, and how they do things with words, radically politicises language as its effects expose multiple apparatuses of government. A focus on linguistic apparatuses has become connected with other apparatuses of government. In social struggles over identity, difference and belonging, we have witnessed how language in apparatuses of knowledge and power is producing classism, racism, sexism, ableism, ageism. This is radicalising linguistic phenomenology with its focus on the linguistic apparatus. There are many examples of these arguments, but those that are relevant to our purpose here include Shoshana Felman ([1980] 2003) who describes how the speaking body scandalises hegemonic power, Judith Butler who shows how speech acts can be injurious ([1997] 2021) and how bodies become gendered through inhabiting and embodying the ordinary language of gender (1990; 1993), and Eve Kosofsky Sedgwick (2003) who illustrates how ordinary language embodies hegemonic power. The struggles over languages of race, ability, sexuality, masculinity, femininity, indigeneity, coloniality, ecology, and nativity and their habitations and embodiment scandalised their hegemonic uses. We have also witnessed how these struggles provoke intense backlashes that are infelicitously named merely as 'culture wars' when they are social and political struggles over language and its uses for domination. What these struggles reveal is that ordinary language embodies power, produces knowledge, and as Ian Hacking (2002, 99–114) argues, creates peoples and things. As we shall see Michel Foucault (1980), Gilles Deleuze ([1986] 1988), and Pierre Bourdieu (1991) were influential in connecting linguistic phenomenology to the productions of knowledge, power, and subjectivity and addressing questions such as for whom ordinary language is ordinary, whose usage is ordinary or unordinary, and for whom its uses and functions are authorised.

If, as James Tully says, 'many of the central and most enduring struggles in the history of politics have taken place in and over the language of citizenship and the activities and institutions into which it is woven' (2014, 1) then how the language of citizenship develops also becomes a political question. We are now aware of the challenge of ordinary languages against official languages of citizenship. This has been particularly forceful in demonstrating how citizenship is gendered and racialised and how citizenship functions to interpellate people into certain ways of being and becoming citizen subjects. This book is inspired by ordinary language philosophy; by studying the linguistic apparatus associated with other knowledge and power apparatuses, we aim to articulate citizenship as an apparatus of government.

We now ask, 'Whose language is citizenship?' with our focus on how people as both citizens and noncitizens are interpellated in particular ways of becoming political subjects. In theory, the language of citizenship belongs to citizens – a collective body of peoples who constitute a polity – in their everyday lives. This is a meaning of ordinary language. Yet, in practice a more complicated picture of ordinary language emerges. Often people – citizens and noncitizens – who constitute a polity through their acts and practices do not only use the ordinary language of citizenship but are also interpellated by official or authorised languages of citizenship. When people speak diverse political languages of rights, wrongs, justice, injustice, legal, illegal, and so forth, they perform a language of citizenship (in) practice as well as citizenship (in) theory, which, as we shall see, are related but function differently. Whose language is citizenship is determined by who is speaking it, how and where it is spoken, and what uses it is being put to.

We approach this complication with a useful distinction that Michael Freeden (2013) makes between *thinking politically* and *political thinking*. We use this distinction, with some modifications, in developing a concept of citizenship in this book. Thinking politically occurs in practices, situations, and acts where language is used toward achieving specific objectives (and exercising power) whether these objectives are consciously articulated or articulable. This is what we called above ordinary language. Yet, thinking politically also occurs when formulating policies, programmes, visions, arrangements, rules, and norms that function as regulative statements or utterances. Often, thinking politically in dominating practices attempts to regulate what can and cannot be said (and indeed seen and heard) in emancipatory practices. This is also ordinary language, but its structure of authorisation and legitimation constitutes it as an 'official language'. If you like, the official language functions in a similar way to what James Scott calls 'seeing like the state' (1998). Scott (1992) has drawn our attention to covert and overt languages in domination and emancipation and then illustrated how overt languages are often spoken from an authorised governmental point of view as 'seeing like the state' signifies. Thinking politically, dominating and emancipatory practices struggle with each other through language. Thus, we distinguish between thinking politically in dominating practices and thinking politically in emancipatory practices and recognise their struggles even though both are ordinary languages. While we distinguish between these two modes of thinking politically, we make yet another distinction: between thinking politically and political thinking.

While most people are engaged in thinking politically, political thinking is accessible to only those people whose authority (status and position) allows them to engage in production of language broadly defined as all articulable or visible utterances. Political thinking interprets, investigates, codes and decodes, or influences how thinking politically develops, either critically, subversively, messily, and rebelliously in emancipatory practices or in authorised and official uses in dominating practices.

These distinctions between ordinary and official languages of thinking politically and between political thinking are also present in the language of politics of citizenship. Often, thinking politically in emancipatory citizenship practices, citizens and noncitizens use ordinary language to contest the meaning and function of citizenship. And, thinking politically in dominating citizenship practices, official languages develop to capture, discipline, and control ordinary language used by citizens and noncitizens. Conventions of political thinking about citizenship embodies, often uncritically, thinking politically in dominating citizenship practices and can serve as its legitimacy or justification. By contrast, critical political thinking about citizenship reveals the tension between thinking politically in emancipatory citizenship practices and thinking politically in dominating citizenship practices.

We shall dwell on these distinctions and make use of them in developing a concept of citizenship as an apparatus of government, but we should now emphasise that when citizens and noncitizens strike against working conditions, struggle for legalising same-sex marriage or for the rights of transgender peoples, mobilise for social housing, protest against welfare cuts, protest against cuts for employment insurance (or unemployment benefits), challenge criminalisation of solidarity with migrants and refugees, march for social justice or against war, challenge conventional clothing in public spaces, seek affirmative action programmes or demand better healthcare access and services, rebel against climate injustice, they do not necessarily articulate themselves as struggling for the maintenance or expansion of civil, political, and social citizenship. The latter remain as categories of official or authorised languages. Instead, people engage whatever struggles seem most related and closest to their social and political lives and dedicate their time and energy accordingly and construct various ordinary languages. While people may not articulate it in thinking politically in dominating or emancipating struggles, it is, however, important to acknowledge that when people engage in such struggles, whatever differences may separate them in values, principles, and priorities, they are also performing citizenship whether they have a status of citizenship or not. What 'enacting citizenship' signifies is that people perform their rights by asking questions concerning justice, rights, equality, and solidarity in specific situations demanding specific languages to perform effective actions. #MeToo, Black Lives Matter, No One is Illegal, Idle No More, Fridays for Future, Ende Gelände, NiUnaMenos, There is No Planet B are amongst hundreds if not thousands of ordinary, situated, and enacted performances that disrupt hegemonic languages by performing citizenship though often not in its name. How do we make sense of this?

Citizenship functions as the necessary but insufficient condition of these social and political struggles, which develop ordinary languages in and by which people articulate and claim rights. When citizenship involves performing the politics of being with others, negotiating situations, identities, and differences, citizens and noncitizens are articulating themselves as distinct yet like others in their everyday lives; they are asking questions of justice, rights, equality, and solidarity but not necessarily always in given meanings of those terms that are part of being with others. Through these struggles, people develop their sense of their rights as others' obligations and others' rights as their obligations. As Ben Golder (2015) shows, it is necessary to understand rights and obligations as relations rather than properties or substances. Although people may interpret or understand their domains of engagement as being separate from each other in their struggles, occasionally an event or situation may remind everyone that we are performing and transforming the language of citizenship. Our task in articulating a concept of citizenship as an apparatus of government is to give an account of how language of citizenship disappears in struggles over citizenship and dissolves into diverse languages.

There is a gap between the ordinary language of thinking politically in emancipatory citizenship practices and the language of thinking politically in dominating citizenship practices; this gap produces sites and senses of political struggle. This is the gap which we shall explore and expose by showing that when people perform ordinary language of citizenship to challenge and transform official languages, they are also making themselves and others.

Although the transformations of the ordinary language of citizenship intensified in the last 75 years, we shall draw on a deep history of citizenship to develop a concept. We shall indeed situate these transformations of the language of citizenship translated from ordinary language of citizenship (thinking politically about citizenship in emancipatory practices and dominating practices) to analytical language of citizenship (political thinking about citizenship) against the background of a deep history of polities. We shall revisit and resignify how citizenship develops a revolutionary language by reversing citizenship as domination into a revolutionary language of citizenship as emancipation. It is now necessary to briefly review how the conventional arrangement of civil, political, and social rights between citizens and polities have been complicated in the last 75 years.

Although the conventional arrangement was famously articulated by T.H. Marshall ([1949] 1996) as shown in the first column of Table 0.1, numerous other scholars have come to accept and repeat this formulation, which still somehow holds its sway as an official language. This arrangement portrays citizenship as a series of rights from the civil,

Table 0.1 The language of citizenship in the last 75 years

Conventional	Critical	Resignified	Transformed	Revolutionary
Civil	Class	Activist	Intersectional	Transversal
Political	Ability	Affective	Transnational	Planetary
Social	Gender	Digital	Decolonial	
	Racial	Ecological	Transgressive	
	Religious	Feminist		
	Cosmopolitan	Global		
	Eurocentric	Human		
	Orientalist	Indigenous		
	Multicultural	Intimate		
		Postcolonial		
		Postnational		
		Precarious		
		Queer		

political, and social spheres to have developed in the last 200 years as a negotiated settlement between citizens and states. This recognises that civil and political rights may have originally excluded certain social groups such as working classes, women, and racialised and indigenous peoples but insists that citizenship had become a 'universal' right with the admission of women, racialised, and indigenous peoples into citizenship. As the second column illustrates in Table 0.1, radical black (Wells-Barnett [1893] 2014; Du Bois [1935] 2013) and radical feminist (Gouges [1791] 2018; Wollstonecraft [1792] 2010) and radical indigenous scholars (see e.g., Temin 2023) had already questioned the universality of citizenship. Iris Young (1989) was amongst the first, and others followed in critique of citizenship functioning as an institution of class, race, ability, gender, religious, and colonial domination (Anderson and Hughes 2015; Bhambra 2015). Citizenship, this critique showed, was not universal but created a 'civilising' hegemonic figure: white, male, straight, upright, normal, and Christian.

A transformative moment came about 20 years ago when scholars began turning their attention from authorised political thinking to the activities and practices of dominated people performing ordinary languages of citizenship and their situated and enacted languages of justice, rights, equality, and solidarity. Against the grain of dominant political thinking about citizenship, as the third column of Table 0.1 shows, we have seen the proliferation of adjectives that experimented with resignifying citizenship as if to see what would happen to the official language of citizenship itself. The list is too long and growing, but prominent amongst them have been feminist citizenship, black citizenship, queer citizenship, postcolonial citizenship, and ecological citizenship. As ordinary language of citizenship, these terms never became authorised in official languages but nevertheless resulted in numerous acts (in both political and legal senses) that enshrined or embodied their principles in national, international, and human rights laws (Nash 2010).

While the proliferation of these adjectives of citizenship has been a powerful force in challenging the official language of citizenship, it began demonstrating that citizenship simultaneously partitions people into citizens and noncitizens with differentiated and hierarchical rights and obligations (Bloom 2017). If people are caught in various categories of noncitizenship (e.g., migrants, refugees, slaves), life becomes precarious with few (if any) rights. Yet, it also recognises that citizenship affords various rights that enable citizens to enjoy them with relatively few obligations – except of course when citizens are interpellated into second-class citizenship categories (e.g., women, workers, blacks, queers) (Cohen 2009). What we began recognising is that citizenship is a play of both domination and emancipation that involves the struggles of those who want to protect certain privileges and the struggles of those against being caught in either second-class or noncitizen categories.

As the experiments in rearticulating ordinary languages of citizenship proliferated, increasingly lessons learned from the social and political struggles of languages began coalescing into transformative languages. As the fourth column in Table 0.1 shows, these are no longer experiments in adjectives but begin enacting what emancipatory languages of citizenship might involve. Scholars have documented how activists using ordinary language of citizenship were identifying intersectionality as a principle, the recognition that everybody embodies multiple positions and situations in social and political struggles, and these connect and intersect diverse peoples differently. They also began identifying the importance of transnational dimension of these struggles and the necessity of solidarity across polities and thus challenging citizenship practices dominated by nationalism, statism, and militarism. Simultaneously, the postcolonial critique has identified how ordinary language and the ways in which people inhabit and embody its precepts reproduced coloniality and thus must be decolonised. And that emancipatory citizenship is transgressive citizenship involving refusal, resistance and indeed rebellion. Citizenship as an activist subjectivity in ordinary language of citizenship shows how it is used by assembling rights and obligations for emancipation from domination. This is when the outlines of a concept of citizenship as an apparatus of government began taking shape in political thinking.

What we come to realise powerfully is that, if indeed the distinction we made between thinking politically about citizenship (in both emancipatory and dominating struggles) and political thinking about citizenship is plausible, it is impossible to sustain a position that scholars politically thinking about citizenship are spectators in all these developments. We as scholars are engaged in thinking politically about citizenship and straddle between ordinary and official languages of citizenship with both emancipatory and domination effects. Bringing this distinction to bear on our position makes it necessary to recognise that we are necessarily activist scholars who are both performing thinking politically about citizenship and politically thinking about citizenship. Embracing this tension rather than assuming an imaginary spectatorship has been amongst the most significant developments in citizenship. This is a revolutionary moment in ways in which we shall articulate in this book.

This book is about articulating a concept of citizenship as an apparatus of government for partitioning, individuating, and aggregating peoples and the struggles for domination and emancipation that proceed from it. We aim to articulate a concept of citizenship that is both capable of accounting for the dominating effects of this apparatus and its emancipatory possibilities through key sites of struggle. To put it differently, we are articulating a concept of citizenship as a revolutionary subjectivity learning from transversal and planetary movements. If we are proposing a concept of citizenship as an apparatus of government, we must now discuss the ways in which we use 'apparatus' and 'government' before we proceed. The concept *dispositif* was used by Foucault and it is translated from French most often as 'deployment', but also as 'apparatus', 'layout', 'device', 'construct', and 'organization' (Elden 2016, 53). As Elden says none of these is adequate to render *dispositif* into English with any precision. But of course, its proposed English counterparts are just as polysemic and unstable so any choice would need justification. To avoid this some scholars continue to use *dispositif* when writing in English. We shall use apparatus rather than *dispositif* but justify its multiple uses. We also need to emphasise that apparatus is strongly associated with how Foucault studied government as an activity rather than the state or polity as such. Foucault says that while for most of its history 'government' in ordinary and official languages meant, for example, governing children, women, patients, and soldiers, only about 500 years ago government became associated specifically with the state as a polity. Using 'government' in a broader historical sense, Foucault insists that overall 'one never governs a state, a territory, or a political structure. Those whom one governs are people, individuals, or groups' ([2004] 2007, 122). By shifting our focus from governing polities to peoples, Foucault, to our knowledge, never suggests that state, territory, or polity are irrelevant but that these arise from the activity of government that produces knowledge, power, and subjects through apparatuses of governing peoples. So when we use apparatus, we always associate it with the activity of governing peoples. Following Foucault, Giorgio Agamben elaborated upon the use of apparatus in relation to government. He invited us to imagine 'a massive partitioning of beings into two large groups or classes: on the one hand, living beings (or substances), and on the other, apparatuses in which living beings are incessantly captured' (Agamben [2006] 2009, 13). Agamben says, always a class of subjects results from the struggle between living beings and apparatuses. An apparatus of government involves '... the capacity to capture, orient, determine, intercept, model, control, or secure the gestures, behaviours, opinions, or discourses of living beings' ([2006] 2009, 14). If we remind ourselves that the relations between polities and peoples began about 6,000 years ago, it is obvious that there have been apparatuses of government throughout this history. But Agamben will insist that modern apparatuses of government in the last 200 years became ubiquitous: he will say that it is difficult to find a situation where the life of beings is not governed by some apparatus (Agamben [2006] 2009, 15). As Tom Frost (2019) notes, there are differences of emphasis in how Foucault and Agamben use 'apparatus'. While the former emphasises its heterogenous elements of assemblage (and hence its possibilities of emancipation) the latter focuses on its functions (and hence its modes of domination). This difference is important as we are interested in citizenship as an apparatus of government that functions for *both* domination and emancipation.

If being governed by an apparatus does not mean being only dominated by it – although that is always a possibility – how do we understand apparatuses of government in their interrelated uses for domination and emancipation? Agamben often emphasises that 'at the root of each apparatus lies an all-too-human desire for happiness. The capture and subjectification of this desire in a separate sphere constitutes the specific power of the apparatus' ([2006] 2009, 17). How does an apparatus produce governable subjects and organise possibilities for both domination and emancipation? When asked how we can study apparatuses, Foucault presents apparatus as an *assemblage* of heterogeneous official and ordinary statements, institutions, buildings, regulations, rules, scientific statements, and propositions, connections that might exist amongst these elements, and urgency that focuses them on subjects of government (1980, 195). Deleuze who elegantly and effectively mapped Foucault's studies on apparatuses: knowledge, power, and subjectivity as lines that cross every apparatus of government as an assemblage ([1989] 2006, 338). Deleuze sees these lines traversing peoples as subjects of domination or emancipation ([1989] 2006, 342). Since the language of lines and fractures are crucial in articulating a concept of citizenship, and since, as Luis de Miranda (2013) shows, Deleuze was only suggestive, we will need to dwell on these terms to indicate how we use them.

Deleuze identifies four lines that constitute an apparatus: visibility, utterance, force, and subjectivation. Each line is closely combined with the others but each can be untangled (Deleuze [1989] 2006, 340). An apparatus renders things visible or invisible (visibility) and it renders words sayable or unsayable (utterance). If its lines of force are invisible and unsayable, these lines can also be rendered visible and sayable. If this happens the lines of subjectivation acquire force. The possibilities of emancipation are entangled with the production of subjectivity escaping the powers and knowledges of one apparatus to reinvest themselves in an another through other forms to be created (Deleuze [1989] 2006, 342). Deleuze will say that 'apparatuses are therefore composed of lines of visibility, utterance, force, subjectivation [but also] breaking and ruptures that all intertwine and combine together where some augment the others or elicit others through variations and even mutations of the assemblage' ([1989] 2006, 342). Since we belong to these apparatuses and act in them exploring their assemblage, their variations and mutations, their stratifications and sedimentations will be required for lines of flight as emancipation (Deleuze [1989] 2006, 345–6). The methodological question that arises is how do we identify these lines? They often become visible once fractures appear in the apparatus: traversing fragmented, distributed, and heterogenous places of tension and moments of fissure. We can plot these lines as fractures that (just barely) hold an apparatus together as an assemblage.

Deleuze is emphatic that 'whether we are individuals or groups, we are made up of lines and these lines are very varied in nature' (Deleuze and Parnet [1977] 2002, 124). Each of the lines that constitute an apparatus of power, knowledge, or subjectivity can have three qualities: segmentary, supple, and flight. The segmentary lines are rigid and Deleuze gives examples as pairs such as family–profession, family–school, family–army, and family–work. These multiple segments cut individuals or groups across multiple rigid lines. The supple lines can bend and enable more refined becomings such as becoming a teacher, a barrister, a judge, an accountant and so on. The supple lines differ in their rhythms and crossings with segmentary lines as they enable certain degrees or quanta of freedom. The third line is a special line for Deleuze as he designates it as a line of flight when it carries those who act toward the unknown, inexistent, and unpredictable. If indeed the line of flight manages to detach from other lines, it appears as a flight from the coercive and disciplinary requirements of the segmentary and supple lines. The line of flight is a rupture as a movement where an individual or a group moves their position in the assemblage not by breaking away from it but by shifting it (127).

The segmentary lines produce binary classifications such as masculine–feminine, child–adult, black–white, public–private, us–them, and, of course, as we shall see, citizen–noncitizen. Deleuze calls these binary machines; they are complex because they cut across, collide with and confront each other, and people are made up of various combinations of these binary machines. The segmentary lines are the basic elements of an apparatus or assemblage where Deleuze credits Foucault for analysing with precision such as prisons, schools, asylums, and hospitals (129). These apparatuses, when assembled, 'organise the dominant languages and knowledge, conformist actions and feelings, the segments which prevail over the others' (129). The lines of flight always arise unexpectedly and disrupt binary machines not by introducing another segment but by tracing another line in the middle of existing binary lines and carries them off according to the variable speeds in a movement of light (131).

These three lines are always caught up with each other. Deleuze insists on the importance of these lines for understanding how individuals and groups are governed by apparatuses. For Deleuze the object of study is neither words nor things but apparatuses as assemblages that produce them: 'utterances do not have as their cause a subject which could act as a subject of enunciation, any more than they are related to subjects as subjects of utterance' (51). This is because 'the utterance is the product of assemblage – which is always collective, which brings into play within us and outside us populations, multiplicities, territories, becomings, affects, events' (51). Deleuze insists his studies on micropolitics, schizoanalysis, pragmatics, rhizomatics, or cartography signify different names but study the same object: lines that cut (rigid), crack (supple), and rupture (flight) individuals or groups (125).

The study of these lines involves understanding the dangers of destroying the rigid lines quickly or slowly, the fluxes of the supple lines, and the thresholds of their rupture. It also involves understanding how these lines partition, individuate, and aggregate peoples.

Deleuze will say that Foucault was unable to develop the concept of apparatus further, but the conditions under which apparatuses generated possibilities of emancipation or how knowledge, power, and subjectivity were fractured by lines (rigid, supple, and flight) remained as promises of this concept. We have seen in the last 30 years numerous studies on security, territory, health, wealth, incarceration, and others as apparatuses of government, and Deleuze himself made contributions along those lines ([1990a] 1995; [1990b] 1995).

We now need to see how we gather these propositions for articulating a concept of citizenship as an apparatus of government. Table 0.2 provides an

Table 0.2 Apparatuses of government: domains and effects

	Production	Knowledge	Power	Subject
Production	Things	Images Signs Sounds Words	Engineering Extraction Factories Machination	Affect Emotion Feeling Sense
Knowledge	Media	Discourse	Authority Law Legitimacy Rights	Abnormal Dangerous Safe Risky
Power	Manufacture	Language	Conduct	Desire Discipline Health Punishment
Subject	Body	Security	Citizenship	People

indicative overview of the relations between apparatuses of government, their effects, and various lines that cut across them. The table is based on a lecture where Foucault (1988) reviews the previous 25 years of his work and attempts to provide an outline. We shall discuss his overview in more detail later as he describes four technologies of government, but here we provide a modified and reconfigured version. The four domains are presented as a matrix of relations. The diagonal parts indicate what each domain creates (things, discourse, conduct, people), lower parts indicate apparatuses of government crossed by each domain (media, manufacture, language, body, security, citizenship), and upper parts indicate how each apparatus creates its effects. The table here indicates the immense complexity of governing people in polities with apparatuses and their effects. Our problem is to place citizenship as an apparatus of government somewhere within this complication and devise ways of theorising its fractures and lines. We will do this by generalising the table against the background of a history of polities.

We have the first evidence of the apparatuses of governing peoples organised as polities from about 6,000 years ago, which was when the city of Uruk in Mesopotamia became the largest and most organised city in the world with up 50,000 inhabitants (Scott 2017, 100). And as Scott says we have enough evidence of other cities such as Kish, Nippur, Isin, Lagash, Eridu, and Ur having developed similar apparatuses of government as Uruk (2017, 119). This means that with the invention of cuneiform speech the apparatuses of government of subjects with administration, regulation, record-keeping, and taxing were already present in these polities. As these polities were transformed and mutated back and forth as cities, states and empires, we have scant evidence to justify calling subjects under their governments 'citizens' although there is evidence of incipient citizenship (Emberling, Clayton, and Janusek 2015, 306). This does not mean that we may not discover evidence of apparatuses of citizenship either under that name or another. But citizenship was named as such in ancient Greek polities about 2,500 years ago for governing peoples, groups, and individuals through partitioning, individuating, and aggregating them. This marks an originary moment, but we must proceed with caution. There are of course multiple apparatuses such as security or territory, but citizenship is amongst the most complicated apparatuses of government as it intersects, combines, and integrates with several others. This is because it transforms subjects and citizens with capacities to obey, resist, subvert, rebel, and struggle *with* citizenship as an apparatus of government and its related and intersecting apparatuses. Until we have further evidence of apparatus of citizenship in ancient polities, we will consider ancient Greek polities as the *naming* of this apparatus rather than its *birth* as it inherits related apparatuses of government in ancient polities.

Table 0.3 shows moments from world history through which we can plot or trace lines of citizenship as an apparatus of government. What Deleuze says about subjectivity as a line of force that is neither reducible nor identical to knowledge or power is crucial for approaching citizenship as an apparatus of government. Subjectivity is the line of force that transforms people into speaking and acting subjects in an apparatus. Subjectivity involves '… individuation that effects groups or people and eludes both established lines of force and constituted knowledge' (Deleuze [1989] 2006, 341). Subjectivity arises from the apparatus as a line of flight. Deleuze says that Foucault understood the ancient Athenian polis as the originary apparatus for subjectivity.

Table 0.3 Citizenship as an apparatus of government: major acts of citizenship

Date	Era	Event
4000	BCE	City of Uruk
3200	BCE	Cuneiform record keeping
2600	BCE	Cuneiform speech acts
2112	BCE	Ur III
594	BCE	Solon, an Athenian governor oversees the entry of the poor into politics as citizens and the cancellation of their debts
508	BCE	Cleisthenes, the principle of equality
91	BCE	Social War, the demands for Roman citizenship of the excluded
212	CE	Citizenship Law, granting citizenship to all 'free' subjects Roman citizenship
1381	CE	Peasant Rebellions
1688	CE	Glorious Revolution, shifting locus of sovereignty
1776	CE	Declaration of Independence, shifting locus of sovereignty
1789	CE	Declaration of the Rights of Man and of the Citizen, shifting locus of sovereignty
1791	CE	The Haitian Revolution, a slave and decolonial revolution
1835	CE	Municipal Corporations Act
1848	CE	European Revolutions
1871	CE	Paris Commune
1917	CE	Russian Revolution
1948	CE	Declaration of Human Rights
1989	CE	East European Revolutions
2011	CE	Arab Revolutions

The polis invents subjectivity as a line of force where being subject to apparatus is a rivalry. Deleuze insists on describing the subject that was invented by the Athenian polis as 'free man'. By replacing 'free man' with citizen we can summarise his insight as follows. From subjectivity as a line of force in which citizens have command over themselves and others, a new line of force or a separate path emerges where the one who commands citizens must also be master of their own subjectivity. This gives rise to a new subjectivity, an autonomous subjectivity, and constitutes new lines of knowledge and power as lines of force. It is this possibility of autonomous subjectivity that enables those who were subjected to this apparatus to overturn its effects and produce lines of flight. If this reminds you of that often repeated, cited, and reiterated description of (ancient) citizenship as the capacity to rule and being ruled, as Aristotle expressed it, we shall see that citizenship as an apparatus of government will prove more complicated, if enigmatic, than this image implies.

What these moments exemplify and signify are revolutions as major acts of citizenship that rupture the principles by which citizenship as an apparatus of government partitions, individuates, and aggregates peoples. If assembling citizenship as an apparatus of government provokes power relations of both domination and emancipation and struggles over it take place in law, theory, practice, and acts as distinct sites and over various meanings of it through which people become its objects and subjects, then we need to develop it as a concept. Undoubtedly, the events marked in Table 0.3 are major acts of citizenship as they are ruptures that open citizen subject as a question.

In Table 0.4 we include some minor acts of citizenship during a 400-year period. We can contrast it with a much larger number of events compiled by Immanuel Ness (2009). Even though Ness covers only the last 500 years or so and only some of the more notable uprisings, revolts, rebellions, and struggles, the evidence of resistance against repressive and oppressive apparatuses, partitioning, individuating, and aggregating peoples is remarkable. Just imagine if we were able to compile evidence of acts of resistance as Peter Weibel (2015) has compiled them for the last 20 years for the last 500 or even 2,500 years. We would have an unfamiliar perspective on major and minor acts of citizenship. We will discuss the reasons why we have separated major and minor acts of citizenship in these two tables when we reflect on citizenship as a revolutionary subjectivity. We should note, however, that major and minor do not imply their importance, but only their performative force as utterances. Some major acts may have minor effects and minor acts major effects. We are concerned with how these lines of flight traverse lines of knowledge, power, and subjectivity. Can we consider all major and minor acts as acts of citizenship? We address this

Table 0.4 Citizenship as an apparatus of government: minor acts of citizenship (after 1500 CE)

Date	Era	Event
1516	CE	Comuneros revolt
1525	CE	German peasant rebellion
1553	CE	Negro Miguel rebellion, first revolt by Africans enslaved by Spain
1571	CE	Túpac Amaru and Incas rebel against Spanish
1606	CE	Bolotnikov, Russian peasant rebellion
1648	CE	French Fronde Revolts
1670	CE	Russian Razin rebellion
1675	CE	American Bacon's rebellion
1687	CE	Yamassee people's revolt, Florida
1707	CE	Russian Bulavin rebellion
1712	CE	Slave revolts, New York colony
1739	CE	Stono rebellion, South Carolina
1741	CE	Slave revolts, New York City
1780	CE	Tupac Amaru indigenous revolts
1798	CE	Ireland rebellions
1819	CE	Manchester Peterloo Massacre
1820	CE	Glasgow general strike
1837	CE	Canadian rebellions
1839	CE	Welsh Chartist revolts
1847	CE	Mayan uprisings
1871	CE	Nyasaland uprisings, South Africa
1878	CE	Kanak uprisings
1886	CE	Haymarket riots, Chicago

question when we discuss citizenship as a revolutionary subjectivity. Whether these acts name it explicitly or assume implicitly, they rupture citizenship as an apparatus of government partitioning, individuating, and aggregating peoples by cutting them through lines of knowledge, power, and subjectivity. These moments are lines of flight that illustrate how people make rights claims on how they are partitioned, how they are individuated, and how they are aggregated.

This is not a book on history of citizenship. We are aiming to articulate a concept of citizenship as an apparatus of government performed by peoples (including activists, artists, scholars, and scientists) who sought to transgress, overcome or transcend the limits of the dominant meanings and uses of citizenship to subvert it for emancipatory practices. We want to articulate this concept as a collective and collaborative development, if not a movement, considering agreements, disagreements, intersections, overlaps and indeed paradoxes that constitute it. We are interested in identifying key fractures of citizenship as an apparatus of government that assembles it, how it is assembled together across sites of law, theory, practice, and acts, and how it provokes struggles for rights for emancipation to resist obligations that sustain domination. We are especially interested in diagnosing how fractures of citizenship open possibilities for revolutionary subjectivity.

Chapter 1

The fractures of citizenship

The struggles over citizenship indelibly mark our present. For about 200 years, whether it is a question of the rights of animals, children, gays, indigenous peoples, lesbians, migrants, minorities, mothers, mountains, paupers, plants, prisoners, protesters, refugees, rivers, robots, slaves, transgender peoples, trees, women, or workers and whether the rights of these subjects are recognised, protected or guaranteed by national laws, international laws, supranational laws, or human rights laws and indeed whether these rights should be conceived as citizenship rights at all have become intense political questions. One way or another these subjects have written themselves into history as citizen subjects. This may not be an exception. As Tully (2014) reminds us, many struggles in the history of politics have taken over the language of citizenship. Yet, it is difficult to overlook the fact that we are experiencing an intensification of struggles over citizenship borne out of the reconfiguration of polities, territories, sovereignties, and movements that render holding citizenship status precarious for some and precious for others and involve not only peoples but also other species of Planet Earth. The present may not be an exception, but it is a transformative moment. With the mass movement of peoples across (and indeed soon beyond) Planet Earth, intensification of the effects of climate change and especially its effects on the movement of peoples, with the emergence of cyberspace extimately and intimately weaving together peoples, places, and things into webs of affiliations, disaffiliations, and surveillance, and with war as a permanent condition, citizenship, as an apparatus invented for governing peoples, is coming apart and held together simultaneously. It is necessary to distinguish the parts that have so far sustained this apparatus, the parts that are coming apart, and the parts that are being held together before we outline a critical perspective on reassembling or dismantling this apparatus.

The central part of this apparatus is the citizen subject who is traversed by multiple lines of visibility, utterance, force, and subjectivation, and

DOI: 10.4324/9781003395997-2

sometimes, of flight. We mentioned earlier that citizenship as an apparatus of government embodies fractures that identify the lines that constitute, assemble, and hold this apparatus together. Through a consideration of the citizen we inherit as a subject intertwined or tangled with colonial, imperial, and national histories, we identify five fractures that render citizenship sensible and intelligible as an apparatus of government. These fractures are movement, technology, coloniality, sovereignty, and planetarity. These fractures cross nomadic–sedentary, episteme–techne, eastern–western, ancient–modern and human–nonhuman not as opposites but as lines that traverse the citizen subject, partitioning, individuating, and aggregating them as peoples into the apparatus.

We begin with tracing lines that render the citizen as a subject of an apparatus of government. These fractures appeared over centuries, but they have been recently exposed as questions of movement, technology, coloniality, sovereignty, and planetarity that traverse the citizen subject. If we consider the citizen subject as a composite of multiple forces, identifications, affiliations, and associations, if indeed the citizen subject is traversed by multiple lines, we must sharpen these lines to identify the parts that have so far sustained this apparatus, the parts that are coming apart, and the parts that are being held together. If we also consider the citizen subject as a composite of multiple forms of power (sovereign, disciplinary, regulatory, and sensory), the citizen subject embodies multiple dispositions (obedience, submission, subversion). By starting with the concept citizenship as an apparatus of government and its fractures, we want to understand how an assemblage of logics, images, symbols, words, and sounds constitute the citizen subject.

Nomadic and sedentary / movement

The line across nomadism and sedentarism traces a fracture of citizenship as an apparatus of government. As Deleuze and Guattari ([1980] 1987) remarked, histories of government have always been written from the perspective of sedentary peoples seeing nomadic peoples as barbarians. The recent contribution of James Scott (2017) to our understanding of the origins of the state as a sedentary polity written from the perspective of nomadic peoples has been, in many ways, a major development of this insight by Deleuze and Guattari.

Scott (2017) says it is not that there were no sedentary peoples before the organisation of the state but that the traditional histories have been written from the perspective of sedentary or state peoples. We have inherited these histories for 500 years and especially in the last 200 years. We now habitually associate cities, states, and empires with civilisation and culture and know life only as partitioned, individuated, and aggregated into such polities. Over time words such as growth, development, and progress have been added to the vocabulary of sedentism. When we view things from the point of view of nomadic or nonstate peoples, we begin to question sedentism. Scott playfully but seriously designates nonstate peoples generically as barbarians and provides an account of the domestication of nonstate peoples into state peoples from about 12,000 years ago to about 4,000 years ago (Scott 1992; 2009). Scott argues that the emergence of polities in fertile valleys across Planet Earth about 6,000 years ago cannot be merely attributed to the invention of cultivation as traditional histories written by state peoples would have it. The invention of the state preceded cultivation by thousands of years and sedentism did not directly or necessarily led to apparatuses of government. Scott challenges the narrative that agriculture was a revolution in food production, freeing people to engage in other pursuits by settling in cities and states. Nor does he suggest that early states provided anything that is implied by civilisation. On the contrary, early states were apparatuses of capture of subject peoples by slavery, bondage, and war. Scott provides a perspective from nonstate peoples outside or at the edges of the state (2017, xii). By bringing nonstate peoples into political thinking about the state specifically and all polities (cities, states, empires), Scott proposes that the domestication of animals and domestication of peoples by states were related: slaves, subjects, and women were effects of such domestication. The French title of his book *Homo Domesticus* ([2017] 2019) captures the essence of his argument that the invention of the state was the invention of domination over peoples and species.

Scott's reinterpretation of the conventional history of the state, which has been told by generations of historians over the last 200 years or so as a progression from nomadism to sedentism can be seen in several ways. It can be seen as an interpretation of history from the perspective of movement rather than settlement. His reversal of sedentism versus nomadism serves this purpose. It is a history from the perspective of nomadism and movement. As Scott rightly insists, our knowledge of history is vastly overpowered by sedentism because it is sedentism that stores, archives, collates, assembles, interprets, and transmits history from its perspective. By contrast, nomadism, peoples at the edges of or outside the state, has not produced a similar durable knowledge and infra- and superstructures for obvious reasons. Polities function as apparatuses for capturing subject peoples and for accumulating surplus for the maintenance and expansion of territories and influence. This is an apparatus that, while it did not invent it, reworks domestication of peoples by peoples and all its variations: slavery, debt bondage, forced labour, forced settlement, forced displacement, and war. Another reading of Scott is his insistence that these polities were fragile apparatuses. They were never all-too-powerful apparatuses and they often and violently collapsed. Yet these collapses have always been interpreted from the perspective of sedentism as catastrophic. From the perspective of nomadism, the periods of these collapses could also have been evidence of emancipation. Finally, sedentism and nomadism are not mutually exclusive, isolated, and independent movements. They depend on each other and produce effects through each other. Sedentism produces nomadism and nomadism consumes sedentism. Or, as Deleuze and Guattari say nomadism and sedentism are immanent and traverse each other. Nomadism is a movement, a becoming that affects sedentism, just as sedentism is a stoppage that captures nomadism (Deleuze and Guattari [1980] 1987, 430).

There is much that fracture reveals for understanding the subsequent history of polities and their apparatuses of government. The rapidly changing interpretations of the beginnings of polities (cities, states, kingdoms, empires) about 6,000 years ago and their mutations show that interpretations of world history and earth history offered in the past 200 years are being deconstructed. Understanding governing peoples through movements involving both sedentism and nomadism as implicating each other rather than opposites is now necessary.

The originary citizenship as an apparatus of government drew not only a virtual but also an actual line between sedentism and nomadism, one that associated the former with property and partitioned property owners from the propertyless as early as the naming of citizenship 2,500 years ago. It individuated people as autochthonous subjects and aggregated them into a territory. The naming of the citizen subject comes with that history. The line fracturing sedentism and nomadism is today as wide as it was when the citizen subject was invented. We experience this fracture in apparatuses that have been assembled to regulate and govern movements of peoples across Planet Earth for protecting state peoples against nonstate peoples. How citizenship as an apparatus of government partitions peoples as autochthonous peoples (we, the people) *with* history and nomadic peoples as peoples *without* history is what undergirds the naming of the citizen subject.

Techne and episteme / technology

Citizenship as an apparatus of government embodies technologies of capturing, classifying, counting, detaining, encamping, enumerating, interning, sequestering, and training peoples. These technologies involve *episteme*: knowing how to govern the conduct of individuals and groups, which we call making of peoples. They also involve *techne*: making of things. Often political thinking keeps these two as separate if not unrelated processes. Citizenship as an apparatus of government involves both making of peoples and things. We provided earlier a modified and reconfigured overview of apparatuses of government, domains of operation, and their effects in Table 0.2 based on how knowledge, power, and subjectivity are entwined with specific technologies (Foucault 1988, 18). But the use of the term 'technologies' does not only mean making of things. Technologies also involve episteme, understood as knowing how to govern peoples. Foucault identified four domains of government in which diverse technologies emerge. First, technologies of production that involve manipulation and shaping of material things. Second, technologies of communication that involve the transmission and codification of images, ideas, symbols, and signs. Third, technologies of power that involve affecting, manipulating, controlling, or dominating the conduct of others. Fourth, technologies of the self that involve acting on our own bodies and souls, thoughts, conduct to transform ourselves to happiness, purity, wisdom, perfection, or immortality (Foucault 1988, 18). These technologies do not develop separately, but each implies a particular form of domination, control, or mastery over their domains. When each works with another, the resultant relations assemble specific apparatuses of government. Foucault, for example, considers Karl Marx as working on the relationship between technologies of production of things and technologies of power where the changes in the former require modification in the latter. Foucault presents much of his work as the relationship between technologies of power and technologies of the self. Although Foucault did not say more about other relationships, let alone the apparatuses that were assembled in them, we need to remind ourselves of this complexity. Table 0.2 cautions us how to theorise citizenship as an apparatus of government related to but distinct from other apparatuses of government embodying both techne and episteme. We shall demonstrate this with a discussion of the invention of corporation as a juridical-political technology that had immense effect on the subsequent development of states and companies.

Of all the parts of citizenship as an apparatus of government, information and communication technologies of government such as surveillance, tracking, tracing, identifying, and sequestering may seem recent. Yet, citizenship as an apparatus of government involving technologies has a longer history. The very naming of citizenship about 2,500 years ago in ancient Greek polities (cities, colonies, and empires) can be traced to the invention of technologies of war. We can suggest rather emphatically that it was the city as a war machine that named the citizen by enabling the ownership of the means of warfare by various groups across a range of classes from peasants, women, slaves, and sailors (Croix 1993). Becoming warrior-citizens as a revolution against kingship was simultaneously a technological revolution. That warrior-citizen and later soldier-citizen served as prototype citizens with virtues of courage and combat is related to the invention of technologies of warfare and their accumulation and appropriation. Similarly, the revolution of the entry of peasant-citizen into the apparatus of citizenship as a political subject was associated with a revolution in the technology of warfare – from chariots to hoplites (Wood 1997).

Yet, it was about 800 years ago that citizenship as an apparatus of government acquired a juridical-political technology: corporation. The origins of corporation as an apparatus of government are amongst the most significant developments in juridical-political history. As Harold Berman (1983) observed it was revolutionary. It is an apparatus that not only made the modern state possible by organising it as a corporation, or at least as juridical-political corporation, it was also crucial for imperial expansion as territorialised (colonies) and deterritorialised (companies) were created as corporations. As such, of course, corporation arranges the juridical-political infrastructure of capitalism with a key apparatus of government. We will return to this shortly but now a brief overview of its development is necessary.

Otto Gierke ([1880] 1939; [1881] 1900; [1881] 1977; [1889] 1934) most tenaciously traced the history of corporation as sovereign cities from about 800 years ago, back to ancient Mediterranean polities about 2,500 years ago, imperial cities about 2,000 years ago, and forward to modern states about 500 years ago. It was Gierke who showed how the jurists struggled with an apparatus that combined both unity and plurality of subjects, an apparatus that was both a legal entity distinct from its peoples and the individuals who composed it (Canning 1980, 12). The invention of the corporation was a response to the political question: how would it be possible for individuals to act and will, distinct from their individual acts and wills, somehow together as a unity and plurality? The answer to this question pivoted around the authority of the corporation itself: once created, did the corporation act and will as a unity to serve the plurality or was the plurality its unity? Throughout this political thinking and thinking politically about this apparatus numerous propositions were formulated, but Gierke brilliantly distilled them into two: corporation as *persona ficta* where it served unity (domination) or *persona politica* where it served the plurality (emancipation). The rights and obligations of its indivisible part – the citizen subject – fell on this line. Gierke did not present it as such, but this will be recognised as the problem of sovereignty as Eric

Santner (2011) formulates it: does it express popular will – body of citizens – or singular will – body of king?

Max Weber was amongst the first to make use of Gierke's political thinking. Weber made a distinction between two types of corporation, spontaneous (*persona politica*) and derived (*persona ficta*), which follows Gierke but generalises it. For Weber the spontaneous corporation emerges as a political association of citizens in defiance of theocratic and royal powers. The sovereignty resides in a body of citizens unified as a corporation. Weber designates derived corporation as legitimate domination and spontaneous corporation as a non-legitimate domination. This signifies the usurpation of the city as an association by legitimate domination subsumed within the state. The derivative nature of corporation was symbolised by charters or grants of limited and limiting rights being given to cities, guilds, and other associations. The spontaneous corporation emerged about 800 years ago and became a derived corporation about 500 years ago with the development of modern state and its sovereignty (Weber [1921] 1978, 1250). Many large cities were originally constituted as spontaneous corporations through swearing an oath of citizenship (Weber [1921] 1978, 1250–1). Although this juridical-political development was most prominent southern Europe, to differing degrees, it was a European development (Weber [1921] 1978, 1252).

Joseph Canning (1980) studied this complicated legal history where a large number of terms were employed by the jurists to signify corporation: *corpus, communitas, respublica, populus, civitas, collegium*, and *societas*, although the most commonly used generic term was *universitas*. This variety reflected numerous groups governing themselves outside the church and the state which ranged from monasteries, guilds, and cities to companies, leagues, and fraternities. The articulation of the city as a sovereign corporation of peoples autonomous from theocratic and royal powers became the most contentious issue as it was connected with the renaming of the citizen subject. The key concern was how to develop the concept of a body (populus) constituted by citizens whose source of authority and legitimacy – to act and will – was none other than itself. As Gerald Frug (1980) documented, the development oscillated between ascribing sovereignty to citizens or theocracy or royal power for 200 years.

Along the way numerous concepts emerged such as *persona ficta, persona politica*, minor, major and so on for partitioning peoples, individuating them, and aggregating them and placing them under theocratic or royal tutelage. If a corporation were a *persona ficta*, it could only be created by a superior power such as a theocratic or royal power. If it were a *persona politica* then its authority and legitimacy and thus sovereignty would be within itself. Similarly, if a corporation were major, it could act and will as a sovereign. If it were minor, it could act and will only under tutelage. To put it differently, citizenship as an apparatus of government was given its juridical-legal form in these centuries, changing the locus of sovereignty from deterritorialised (guilds, monasteries) to territorialised (cities) and reterritorialised (states) associations.

The history and development the corporation as an apparatus of government is complex and diverse, and its study is scarce. Yet, its significance is immense. The organisation of cities, the renaming of the citizen, and the development of the state are intricately woven into this history. The reason we have discussed it in exploring the fracture between techne and episteme is to reveal how technologies of government – amongst which the corporation is the most important – embody both: the development of episteme of government such as discipline, surveillance, control, and training develop with their associated techne such as guilds, universities, fraternities, schools, asylums, workhouses, factories, companies, and hospitals. We must keep this complex history always in view, but we can mention three significant uses of the corporation: the creation of companies during colonisation, the formation of military companies in modern armies, and the rise of cyberspace corporations for partitioning, individuating, and aggregating deterritorialised peoples.

While it is well known that empires established companies for their early colonisation and that these companies were crucial in their settlement, it is often overlooked that these companies were the same apparatus of government – corporation – that had become ubiquitous in governing guilds, associations, trading companies, cities, and indeed states. The illustrious histories of the Portuguese East India Company, British East India Company, Dutch West and East India Companies illustrate how their corporate structure was *persona ficta*, designed to perform domination at a distance or as an apparatus of deterritorialised government (Bowen 2006; Dalrymple 2019; Phillips and Sharman 2020). Similarly, the increasing use of corporation by contemporary armies relying on private military companies is a significant transformation of ancient and modern citizen armies organised as associations.

The recent development of the internet, the emergence of platforms to partition, individuate, and aggregate peoples and both territorialise and deterritorialise their government also involves legal corporation as an apparatus of government and generates new forms of citizenship that function both as domination and emancipation.

If the development of citizenship as an apparatus of government was entwined with both episteme and techne, making of peoples and things, the emergence of colonising, military, and digital technologies must all be seen in all four dimensions we have illustrated in Table 0.2. The emergence of data empires, for example, whose extraction of data about movements, gestures, and activities of peoples and capturing them as subjects of government constitutes the most striking development affecting citizenship as an apparatus of government. Of most significance is that modern states can no longer hold sovereign power over citizens or at least cannot maintain and sustain it with the new subjectivation of peoples into apparatuses of government controlled by data empires.

Eastern and western / coloniality

We need to understand how the line that fractures two geopolitical names – east and west – also fractures citizenship as an apparatus of government. Although it was Max Weber (1927a) who was most emphatic about drawing this line, modern apparatus of citizenship cites and repeats this line between liberal and illiberal, and democratic and authoritarian political subjectivities and maps them back onto the western and eastern line. A concept of citizenship exposes this line as a fracture between eastern and western polities. We can see how Weber traces the origins of citizenship to ancient Greek and Roman cities organised as fraternities and oath-bound communities, then demonstrates how the apparatus of these polities were revived in European cities 700 and 800 years ago and how modern states inherited them about 400 to 500 years ago. Since this line is a constitutive fracture of citizenship, it is necessary to go over Weber's logic briefly.

Writing about 100 years ago Weber was mostly following contemporary historians in search of the originality of the west as the origins of capitalism rather than the east. Weber was a rare historical sociologist as his explanation was a combination of economic, social, cultural, territorial, and religious developments rather than any single one of them. For Weber, all these developments converged on the city as an originary form. By defining the city as a transhistorical concept since its origins about 6,000 years ago, Weber identified five essential characteristics constitutive of the city (territory, market, autonomy, association, and religion). Weber argued that what made the west unique was that it invented the city as a fraternity, a brotherhood-in-arms for mutual aid and protection, and revolutionary subjectivity or 'usurpation of political power' (1927a, 319). Weber connected the European 'communes' of 900 to 700 years ago and ancient 'synoecism' (settling together) between 2,500 and 2,000 years ago. He was following his contemporaries in describing the origins of cities in the east 6,000 years ago as authoritarian or despotic. Thus, ancient Greek and Roman cities were prototypical cities where citizenship originated and developed centuries later in the west to constitute its uniqueness. Weber generalised the Mediterranean polis as '... always the product of such a confraternity or synoecism, not always an actual settlement in proximity but a definite oath of brotherhood which signified that a common ritualistic meal is established and a ritualistic union formed and that only those had a part in this ritualistic group who buried their dead on the acropolis and had their dwellings in the city' (1927a, 320). This generalisation had both backward and forward effects.

Looking backward, Weber sees the lack of development of the generalised polis in what were then called 'other' civilisations. Weber consistently emphasises that some of these characteristics emerged in China, Japan, the Middle East, India, and Egypt, but he insists that it was only in the west that all were present and appeared regularly. From this Weber concludes that 'most importantly, the associational character of the city and the concept of a [citizen] (as contrasted to the man from the countryside) never developed [in the east] at all and existed only in rudiments' ([1921] 1978, 1227). Therefore '...a special status of the town dweller as a "citizen", in the ancient medieval sense, did not exist and a corporate character of the city was unknown' ([1921] 1978, 1227). He was convinced that

> in sharp contrast to the medieval and ancient [west], we never find the phenomenon in the [east] that the autonomy and the participation of the inhabitants in the affairs of local administration would be more strongly developed in the city ... than in the countryside. In fact, as a rule the very opposite would be true.
>
> ([1921] 1978, 1228)

The conclusion was that 'all safely founded information about Asian and oriental settlements which had the economic characteristics of "cities" seems to indicate that normally only the clan associations, and sometimes also the occupational associations, were the vehicle of organized action, but never the collective of urban citizens as such' ([1921] 1978, 1233). Above all, for Weber the concept of citizen was present only in the west because only in the west did the city exist in the specific sense of a collective body, a people as a whole (1927b, 232). The repeated argument that the east lacked the citizen subject as its smallest indivisible part and city as its polity as a whole was always supported by evidence showing how the necessity of irrigation in arid lands in eastern civilisation produced centralised bureaucracies.

Weber has been criticised by showing the presence of many if not all characteristics of citizenship in other ancient cities (e.g., Dassow 2023; Gerçek 2023). Our focus however is on Weber's performativity. How does his statement function? What does it produce? Constructing a generalised polis, Weber portrays the modern European state as the inheritor of 'ancient' and 'medieval' polities and a bourgeois class as its citizen subject. For Weber, the European state that developed was the polis writ large with appropriate legal and administrative structure. Although Weber has also articulated the iron cage metaphor to describe modern state bureaucracy, he was waxing nostalgic about the direct democracy of polis as opposed to representative democracy of the state. Nonetheless, for Weber the key was that the development of western capitalism was associated with the generalised polis and the state as the guarantor of its legal and administrative infrastructure. Both capitalism and the naming of the citizen subject in Europe were fitted into this imaginary that explained the differences between the backward east and the forward west. What Weber accomplishes is mapping ancient–modern and east–west lines to make citizenship as an apparatus of government an originary apparatus. Yet we will draw these lines differently to expose Weber's unintended colonialism and orientalism.

An irony of this imaginary, which still holds sway, is that colonialism and imperialism remain entirely outside its scope, its point of view. The ancient civilisations that Weber and his followers describe as lacking the characteristics of a generalised polis, and hence the conditions for the development of capitalism and a bourgeoisie as its driving force, included peoples and places that European empires subjected to direct or indirect colonial and imperial rule for more than 500 years. The origins of citizenship may be seen in the generalised polis of 2,500 years ago or even 800 years ago, but its modern features were formed during the emergence of European empires about 500 years ago. After a series of decolonisations and the emergence of the postcolonial state, we now recognise domination from slavery to dispossession as the legacies of colonialism. That such legacies do not often feature in the apparatus of citizenship is all the more revealing as these counter-histories are as old as colonisation itself. If indeed the modern state was the generalised polis writ large, its colonies of direct and indirect rule and peoples whose lives and livelihoods were exploited were its other territories and peoples (women, slaves, merchants) that made the originary polis possible. To put it bluntly, the imaginary of the west as the originator of polis and subsequently of capitalism conceals the imperial origins of the bourgeois citizen subject.

The renaming of the citizen subject can be traced to the colony in the formation of European empires about 500 years ago. Although it was about 200 years ago that it became possible to speak about empires of liberty protecting imperial citizens from tyranny, settling peoples in the colony and governing them at a distance raised again the question of the citizen. To put it differently, the imaginary we discussed above between ancient and modern citizenship was effectively regenerated through imperial practice. As Anthony Pagden shows, this happens in two stages. About 500 years ago, the first stage involves European states creating a close association between a people and its territory, which Weber called synoecism or autochthony. This is also the origin of the idea of popular sovereignty as the authority of a people over a territory. At this stage, both the style of rule and the occupied territory are called dominium. With the opening of colonies with slaves, settlers, and servants, the dominium creates problems for the government of empires: if there is a close association between a people and its territory, dominium both as a style and place of rule, then how can settler colonialism with slaves and servants rule over indigenous peoples? To put it differently, if autochthony gives rights to peoples to govern themselves, by what authority could empires deny it to indigenous peoples? The second stage witnesses the naming of citizenship as an apparatus of government by partitioning peoples into various categories (citizens, settlers, slaves, servants, natives, and aliens), individuating them into various contracts, and aggregating them into diverse hierarchies. Indigenous peoples remain outside these hierarchies as savages and become aggregated with nonhuman species. We can suggest that citizenship as an apparatus of government was born out of imperial domination when it sought to redefine sovereignty. The second stage then understands both the style of rule and territory as not dominium but imperium. Pagden sees the Governor of Massachusetts, Thomas Pownell, revealing this shift. Pownell (1752, 94) writes 'this modelling of the people into various orders and subordinations of orders, so that it be capable of receiving and communicating any political motion, and acting under that direction as a one whole is which the Romans called by the peculiar word imperium'. Pownell says that imperium is the only apparatus through which a people can be partitioned and aggregated into a political body and through which independent particles cohere into a body, and this body does not need to dwell in a singular territory, or rather its territory is not enclosed or contiguous but an expansive territory. For Pownell this is the meaning of imperium as a polity.

A concept of citizenship deconstructs this apparatus and develops a language of struggle between the domination, emancipation, and multiplicities in the emergence of citizenship as an apparatus of government.

The appropriation of Greek and Roman polities and societies as the origins of citizenship and portraying diverse peoples and places by their ostensible lack thereof conceals the fractures of sovereignty and coloniality. But deconstructing this apparatus is not merely a reversal by way of which it is illustrated that indeed diverse peoples developed citizenship that we immediately recognise. Rather, these fractures of citizenship as an apparatus of government must be rendered sensible and intelligible. The struggles for decolonising indigenous peoples have been crucial for understanding the relations between sovereignty and coloniality. Successfully undoing themselves from the hierarchical categories of imperial citizenship such as aboriginals, natives, or first nations, indigenous peoples have brought into being or forced themselves as a historical subject into being indigenous (Alfred and Corntassel 2005). This happened through many struggles and across both practical and theoretical domains. The recovery of subjugated knowledges of indigenous peoples by Taiaiake Alfred (1999), Kiara Vigil (2015), Jodi Byrd (2011), Audra Simpson (2014), and David Temin (2023) reveal how sovereignty and coloniality are underlying and impossible forces of the domination of indigenous peoples by imperial citizenship apparatus. And as Yuko Miki (2018) and Deborah Yashar (2005) show this domination enforced various hierarchies between diverse groups of settlers, slaves, servants, convicts, and indigenous peoples.

After decolonisation of previously colonised peoples and territories from about 150 to 75 years ago, the postcolonial states inherited some of these fractures of citizenship as an apparatus of government. Before colonisation there were thousands of nonstate peoples inhabiting Planet Earth and after colonisation most were captured into about 200 or so states, each with its own citizenship as an apparatus of government (Hindess 1998; Arneil 2007). There are still thousands of nonstate and indigenous peoples inhabiting Planet Earth who are subject to citizenship as an apparatus of government (Minahan 2016). We may well consider this as the continuation of coloniality by means of citizenship as an apparatus of government. As we shall see below, deconstructing the imaginary of the birth of the citizen subject has still more radical consequences.

Ancient and modern / sovereignty

Modern citizenship has an uneasy relationship with ancient citizenship, as it considers everything before itself as ancient and yet constitutes itself (selectively) as its inheritor. This operates with two imaginaries: that modern citizenship is emancipation and that it is universal.

First, modern citizenship imagines itself as a progression from dominated to emancipated citizen subject. It marks modern citizenship as the moment of emancipation from domination or the transformation from being the subject of a sovereign to being a sovereign subject: the citizen subject. The very idea of the citizen subject is an emancipated subject as a sovereign subject.

Second, modern citizenship imagines the citizen subject as a universal subject. Étienne Balibar (2012) says that the modern citizen is a person who enjoys rights in completely realising being human and is free because being human is a universal condition for everyone. This is the sovereignty of the body of citizens or popular sovereignty. Yet, while some subjects are considered as citizens, such as white, male, propertied, able-bodied, Christian, and heterosexual peoples, the opposites of each of those subject positions remain as subjects with limited rights or without rights.

These two imaginaries have been criticised both theoretically and empirically. We shall not dwell on the critiques of domination versus emancipation or universalism versus particularism. But a concept of citizenship we are articulating in this book will show that these imaginaries are implicated in each other, depend on each other, and require each other. By extension ancient and modern are also implicated in each other, and rather than drawing a line between the two, we shall propose a concept of citizenship as an apparatus of government where both ancient and modern strategies and technologies of government are assembled. These strategies and technologies are intertwined forces of knowledge, power, and subjectivation. The apparatus inscribes citizen subject as that person with the right to have rights. For more than 200 years, the citizen subject has acquired certain rights that constitute it: civil, political, and social rights. Civil rights, such as the right to free speech, the right to privacy, the right to due process, freedom from arbitrary power, freedom to associate, the right to dignity, and freedom of conscience, are outcomes of social struggles over these rights and simultaneously required submission to authority and subversion (e.g., dissent, resistance, protest) of that authority. Similarly, political rights, such as the right to vote representatives to the parliament, to run for office, to organise political parties and movements, to protest, to assemble, and to engage in civil disobedience are political rights that overall define the citizen subject. The social rights of citizenship have their history of struggles, too. The right to universal benefits, welfare, allowances, and health and other social services are not only won through social struggles but also establish a principle: the citizen subject, to be affective, must acquire not only a modicum of civil life but also social existence.

Yet, all these instituted rights traverse both ancient and modern forms of citizenship, and rather than opposing ancient and modern, we can draw lines across numerous moments of political history in the form of charters, bills, and declarations claiming rights as shown in Table 0.3. These are by no means comprehensive geographically or historically but are examples of how repeatedly inscribing rights as claims through social and political struggles and how repeating and citing have been both the origins and effects of the making of the citizen subject.

Balibar's formulation is brilliant: the citizen subject is not merely *subject to power* or the *subject of power* but embodies both ([2011] 2017, 46). If being a subject *to* power demands obedience, being a subject *of* power provokes disobedience. These are not pure forms; rather, the apparatus produces these subjectivities as potentialities. Being a subject *to* power is marked by the citizen's domination by the apparatus, and their rights derive from that which is given to them by the (patriarchal) sovereign. Being a subject *of* power means being an agent of power, even if this requires submission. There is a significant difference between obedience and submission. If being *subject to power* means obedience to the sovereign, then it requires domination as a form of power. Whether this is total obedience or resistant obedience depends on the circumstances. By contrast, being a *subject of power* means *submission* to authority in whose formation the citizen subject participates and the potential *subversion* of that authority. What distinguishes the citizen from the subject is that the citizen is this composite subject of obedience, submission, and subversion. The naming of the citizen as a *subject of power* does not mean the disappearance of the subject as a *subject to power*. The citizen subject embodies these forms of power in which it is implicated, where obedience, submission, and subversion are not separate dispositions but are always present potentialities.

Balibar ([2011] 2017) reminds us how Foucault's question about the transformation from ancient to modern forms of power with his emphasis on the simultaneous presence of obedience, submission, and subversion is essential for understanding the fractures of citizenship as an apparatus of government. Expressing the basic question that motivated his studies on power, knowledge, and ethics, Foucault asks, how governing subjects in Western Christian culture demands not only acts of obedience and submission but also acts of freedom (1997, 81). For Foucault, it was acts of freedom that afforded possibilities for subjects to constitute themselves as subjects of power and subjects to power. This also means that acts of freedom afford possibilities of both disobedience and subversion. Being a subject of power means responding to the call 'how should one "govern oneself" by performing actions in which one is oneself the objective of those actions, the domain in which they are brought to bear, the instrument they employ, and the subject that acts?' (Foucault 1997, 87). It was Foucault who developed 'a domain of acts, practices, and thoughts' as a problem of the apparatus of government (1997, 114). Not unlike Deleuze but from a different point of view, Balibar sees Foucault's project as 'the birth of the citizen subject' ([2011] 2017, 55). Balibar says that what concerns Foucault is primarily how subjects become citizens through various processes of subjectivation that involve relations between bodies and things that constitute them as subjects *to* and *of* power. If we focus on how people enact themselves as subjects of power, it involves investigating how people use language to describe themselves and their relations to others and how language summons them as speaking beings. To put it differently, it involves investigating how people do things with words and words with things to enact themselves. It also means addressing how people understand themselves as subjects to and of power when acting. This requires exploring not only how people come into being as speaking subjects who use language but also their other modes of engaging and acting. Balibar locates contradictions in the process of subjectivation, citizen's becoming-a-subject, and the struggles it generates ([2011] 2017, 53).

Both ancient and modern citizen subjects are not only capable of being obedient but can also be simultaneously a submissive (*to* authority) and a subversive (*of* authority) figure. This always carries within it the possibility and danger of the obedient subject of sovereign power. The citizen is a subject who submits to government in which they are implicated. This submission makes the citizen a subject of subversion capable of questioning the terms of their own submission. To put it differently, the performative force of the citizen subject appears in the gap between the capacity to submit to authority and yet the ability to act in dissent. This is not a sovereign subject in the mastery of their destiny, but an embodied subject formed through games of multiple affiliations and of submission and subversion. The rights that the citizen holds are not the rights of an already existing sovereign subject but the rights of a subject who submits to authority in the name of those rights and acts to call into question its terms. This is the tension between submission and subversion of the figure of the citizen that can be expressed as submission *as* freedom.

If a concept of citizenship recognizes that citizens and noncitizens are both subjects *to* power and subjects *of* power and that this involves obedience, submission, and subversion as its dispositions, a more complex apparatus emerges. If indeed the citizen subject comes into being performatively through making rights claims, we inherit all these accumulated dispositions. The conclusion that we can draw from this fracture of citizenship between ancient and modern citizenship, attributing particularism and domination to the former and emancipation and universalism to the latter, these binaries cannot inform a concept of citizenship attuned to its history. This becomes even more imperative when we see the fracture of the apparatus of citizenship between east and west. The question of the sovereignty of the citizen and of the authority that constitutes it cannot be understood without revealing another fracture of citizenship as an apparatus of government: coloniality. If we are seeing the citizen as partitioned, individuated, and aggregated sovereignty, we can also see that it was reinvented in the colony and a fracture between ancient and modern becomes possible only when a line is drawn between eastern and western and ancient and modern polities.

Human and nonhuman / planetarity

Another fracture that the modern apparatus of citizenship tenuously and precariously holds is between human and nonhuman subjects of politics. Let us put this as emphatically as possible: citizenship as an apparatus of government is predicated upon domination of nonhuman species by human species. The modern imaginary of the citizen subject conceals this domination over not only other peoples but also other species. Animals, mountains, rivers, seas, plants, and other species of Planet Earth are not accorded either subjectivity (being subjects to power or subjects of power) or subjectivation (possibilities of becoming subjects). Their domination is signified as the natural order of things. Although the domination of human species over other nonhuman species was questioned at least 500 years ago with resistances by indigenous and enslaved peoples during colonisations, it was astonishingly only about 25 years ago that this domination was named as Anthropocene. It names our geological time as the end of another – Holocene (12,000 years ago) – and the beginning of Anthropocene when human species became the primary agents for climate change and triggering a chain of reactions that threatens its sustainability if not existence.

Whether we date Anthropocene from the use of nuclear power (75 years ago), fossil fuels (200 years ago), European colonisation, enslavement, and capture of indigenous peoples (500 years ago) or from the domestication of animals, plants, and cultivation (12,000 years ago) is being debated. The human species having become the primary agent of climate change, not only through its extractivism but also through militarism and colonialism, is however beyond doubt. A consequence is the emergence of planetary movements where a negotiated settlement of cohabitation between human species and nonhuman species is sought. This alters the meaning of the smallest indivisible part of a polity – citizen subject – as a part of planetary politics. Who are the subjects of citizenship as an apparatus of government? Are we at a moment when we must accept that the citizen subjects cannot be only human species but must include nonhuman species? Are we developing radically transformative relations between human and nonhuman species and between these species and Planet Earth? Are nonhuman species and Planet Earth and indeed other planets moving from the background to the foreground of politics? How has the partitioning of human species into various peoples and peoples into citizens and noncitizens left nonhuman species outside politics?

The fracture between the human and nonhuman is therefore a constitutive structure as it traverses a line that ruptures a 12,000-year history of human domination of Planet Earth and its species. The effects of this rupture on citizenship as an apparatus of government may be immense. Although recent citizenship as an apparatus of government enabled polities (cities, states, empires) for the exploitation of human and nonhuman species and life on Planet Earth, which itself has been relentlessly territorialised (partitioned into states and peoples) and reterritorialised (colonisation of low orbit space and high seas), its peoples have been captured (as slaves, indentured servants) and recaptured (refugees, peons, debtors), and its species are either domesticated or becoming extinct.

We must return to the movements of indigenous peoples as a subject of history and remind ourselves that the movement exposes the fracture of not only sovereignty and coloniality but also planetarity. The indigenous movements began articulating not only a different relationship between indigenous peoples and their dominant others but also a new relationship between human species and nonhuman species and Planet Earth (Bjork-James, Checker, and Edelman 2022). These articulations are simultaneously practical, ethical, political, and aesthetic as they radically recast the question of living well on Planet Earth. Of most significance in these articulations is the question of whether nonhuman beings can become citizen subjects. Can plants, animals, rivers, mountains enter the apparatus as citizen subjects with history?

It was William Connolly who argued that several changes such as climate patterns, drought zones, distressed oceans, extinct species, disappearing glaciers, and violent hurricanes have been reshaped not by 'abstract' human activity but by capitalism, militarism, technologism, and scientism in the last 200 years and this may become the defining moment of the planetary. He stresses that 'today the urgency of time calls for a new pluralist assemblage organized by multiple minorities drawn from different regions, classes, creeds, age cohorts, sexualities, and states' (Connolly 2017, 9). We can of course add to this list all those nonhuman subjects we named above. Must we, and if so, how do we consider human and nonhuman subjects as citizens? Dipesh Chakrabarty suggests that we must now combine earth history and world history. Whether Anthropocene is an epoch or condition, as Chakrabarty argues, it influences how we theorise what we propose here as citizen subjects. This is because '... we are passing through a unique phase of human history when, for the first time ever, we consciously connect events that happen on vast geological scales – such as changes to the whole climate system of the planet – with what we might do in the everyday lives of individuals, collectivities, institutions, and nations (such as burning fossil fuels)' (Chakrabarty 2021, 125). We are also realising that for planetary movements these connections are not only between temporal (geological or historical) horizons but also between and across geographical spaces and it requires understanding these movements not only as historical movements and geographical movements (world history) but also as planetary movements (earth history).

Domination and emancipation / power

These lines of fracture traverse all those who are captured by the apparatus of citizenship who in turn traverse these lines themselves. The lines that trace fractures of apparatuses of government over the past 6,000 years also trace the fractures of the present but differently. We can provide numerous examples. Most obvious are indigenous peoples, slaves, and transgender peoples finding themselves being traversed not only by sovereignty and coloniality but also planetarity and thus being constituted by the citizenship apparatus of government as nonhuman subjects or subjects without history. Yet, overturning this hierarchy by traversing the line in the opposite direction they gradually but effectively constitute themselves as peoples with history and subjectivity, resignifying movement, technology, coloniality, sovereignty, and planetarity by recasting their relationship with Planet Earth.

What we have revealed through these fractures are lines that citizenship as an apparatus of government traverses: domination and emancipation. If the exercise of power means influencing shaping, and guiding the conduct of ourselves and others, as Foucault always insisted, domination and emancipation are modalities of power that embody and implicate each other. As Ernesto Laclau (2007) shows emancipation evokes multiple and often contradictory meanings, but emancipation as a condition which precedes an act of emancipation captures our meaning as a line of flight, as a possibility, or as Scott (1992) would put it, as a breakthrough from domination. There is never oppression, repression, or submission without emancipation, and conversely, there is never liberation without domination. They do not exist as polar opposites where one begins and the other ends. We cannot ascertain how an apparatus serves or functions for one or the other without taking it apart. As Brandzel (2016) warns us often scholars are compelled to make a normative choice between domination or emancipation. Michael Mann (1987) and Bryan Turner (1986; 1990) exemplify two opposites. For Mann citizenship is an apparatus of domination, as it embodies ruling class strategies. For Turner citizenship is an apparatus of emancipation, as it embodies possibilities for rights. For Turner (1990, 189) 'a conservative view of citizenship (as passive and private) contrasts with a more revolutionary idea of active and public citizenship'. Both are right as long as we hold these positions together because citizenship as an apparatus of government functions as neither an apparatus of domination only nor emancipation only. Charles Tilly thought that he could evade this commitment since any normative investment in citizenship is dangerous (1997, 599, 607). By designating government as any organisation that controls the coercive means in a given polity, Tilly considers citizenship as a relation between governmental agents acting uniquely as such and whole categories of persons identified uniquely by their connection with the government in question (509). For Tilly citizenship then involves claims relating categories of persons to agents of governments (600). For Tilly citizenship has the character of a contract: 'variable in range, never completely specifiable, always depending on unstated assumptions about context, modified by practice, constrained by collective memory, yet ineluctably involving rights and obligations sufficiently defined that either party is likely to express indignation and take corrective action when the other fails to meet expectations built into the relationship' (1997, 600; 1995, 8). Unlike other contracts, however, citizenship binds whole categories of persons rather than single individuals to each other, involves differentiation among levels and degrees of members, and directly engages a government's coercive power. These three aspects of citizenship make it a potent form of contract and generated serious struggles for centuries over military service, eligibility for public office, voting rights, payment of taxes, public education, access to public services, and protection of rent-producing advantages (Tilly 1997, 600). In other words, the citizen subject was a proprietor, legislator, magistrate, selector, and soldier.

Tilly recognises the variations of the contracts between citizens and states and suggests it is impossible to create a permanent boundary between citizens and noncitizens. Tilly observes that 'all states differentiate within their citizenries, at a minimum distinguishing between minors and adults, prisoners and free persons, naturalized and native-born' (1997, 601). Moreover, all states introduce gradations such as 'restricting suffrage or military service to adult males, imposing property qualifications for certain rights, or installing a range from temporary residents to probationary applicants for citizenship to full-fledged participants in citizenship's rights and obligations' (1997, 601). Is Tilly close to recognising citizenship as an apparatus of government? The language of contract distracts from understanding the apparatus in its enabling structure of struggle by subversion and resistance. Moreover, as we shall see when we discuss J.L. Austin on performative utterances, as much as Tilly wishes to distinguish between analysis, description, and advocacy, speech acts are always performative and contain elements of all three utterances.

Mann focuses on the coercive means by which the ruling class governs citizens. Turner reveals the ways in which resistance brings about change. And Tilly shows how claims and counterclaims between governments and citizens are the constitutive parts of struggles over citizenship. Although Mann, Turner, and Tilly emphasise various aspects of citizenship as an apparatus of government, it is necessary to see all these aspects assembled together and how power relations fracture the apparatus.

If citizenship governs the relationship between a polity, its peoples, and its species, by partitioning them into citizens (strangers), noncitizens (foreigners, aliens), and nonhuman (abjects) with or without rights and obligations, individuating them with attributes and characteristics, and aggregates them by classifications, it also opens possibilities for objection, resistance, protest, or struggle. If people are caught in various noncitizen categories (e.g., migrants, refugees, slaves), life becomes precarious with few (if any) rights. Yet citizenship affords various rights that enable citizens to enjoy them with few obligations – except of course when citizens are in second-class citizenship categories. Citizenship as an apparatus of government functions then as an apparatus of domination and emancipation that brings into play the struggles of those who want to protect certain privileges and the struggles of those against being caught in either second-class or noncitizen categories. That citizenship is an apparatus of government whose institution involves both domination and emancipation raises questions on how it functions. This we address by first outlining the sites of struggle through which it is assembled and then how these struggles render sensible and intelligible the utterances of, in, and by which it functions.

Chapter 2

The sites of enacting citizenship

If citizenship as an apparatus of government traverses the relations between peoples (subjects, citizens, noncitizens) and polities (cities, states, companies, empires, leagues, federations) and how peoples identify or affiliate with or are subjugated in polities, it involves distinct but overlapping sites of struggle through which this apparatus is assembled. By the assemblage of citizenship as an apparatus of government we mean the making of the smallest indivisible part of a polity – citizen subject – by partitioning, individuating, and aggregating peoples, and instituting polities. The primary means by which partitioning, individuation, and aggregation occurs is through rights of the people as a whole and peoples as its parts. The making of the citizen is an effect of citizenship as an apparatus of government. Its assemblage brings into play four sites of performativity, its production and reproduction. They are citizenship (in) law, citizenship (in) practice, citizenship (in) theory, and citizenship (in) acts. These are distinct and overlapping sites of assembling citizenship as an apparatus of government, and they become objects of social and political struggles because each develops distinct performative logics in relation to the others. The work of assembling citizenship as an apparatus of government – the making of the citizen subject – gets done through these distinct but overlapping sites and their multiple functions.

The partitioning, individuating, and aggregating of peoples and making them into citizens follows the five stages of how different kinds of people come into being proposed by Ian Hacking (2002). We shall adapt these five stages as the sites of assembling citizenship as an apparatus of government. Following Foucault and broadly using a performative style of thought, Hacking starts with the proposition that kinds of people are both words and things as effects of each other (Hacking 2002, 3). To understand these effects, we need to understand how kinds of people come into being as both words and things. The words that partition, individuate and aggregate people into things must be seen as dynamic enactments. These words

DOI: 10.4324/9781003395997-3

become sensible and intelligible only as far as we understand how they come into being, acquire their meanings and functions, and produce their effects as things. Hacking says, 'the idea that peoples just separate naturally into overarching racial, ethnic, or linguistic groups is largely a product of a recent invention, the nation state' (Hacking 2007, 289). That this separation is the product of an invention or that peoples are being made up does not mean that those peoples are fictional but that there is a history through which they were created in social and political struggles involving power relations. There is no reason to assume that we will find these words in the past in the same manner describing exactly the same things as we understand by them now or that the words we use now to describe things are evolved versions of words in the past. The word 'invention' draws attention to their historicity. To put this in our words, the 'kinds of people' are invented through citizenship (in) law where people are constituted as acting beings as citizens or noncitizens. These words become embedded in citizenship (in) practice and provide ways of being in citizenship (in) acts. All acts are acts performed of, in, and by words. If new words come into being, new possibilities for action come into being as their consequence (Hacking 2002, 108). It is in this sense that naming a people with words is an act of 'making up a people'. However, unless people take up these words and act upon them and each other, a word would not have any performative force. When people act, they interact with words, and this creates a looping effect where words acquire performative force. The name (word) and the named (thing) dynamically interact. Hacking insists that this process is dynamic in the sense that there is no static moment in the looping effect where the named (thing) can be said to be the effect of the name (word) or vice versa. Instead, the name and the named are constituted dynamically.

Adapting Hacking, we propose five dynamic sites through which citizenship as a word and its partitions, individuations, and aggregations become effects of each other. This is how citizenship as an apparatus of government is assembled. First, words appear about the kinds of people, and these are often codified through citizenship (in) law. Second, people begin to take up these words: citizenship (in) practice. Third, arrangements for managing the kinds of people acting under these words emerge and elicit or provoke resistance or refusal: citizenship (in) acts. Fourth, knowledge about the kinds of people in question appears: their characteristics, obedient or disobedient, active or passive, virtuous or vicious, healthy or unhealthy: citizenship (in) theory. Fifth, authorities, experts, and bureaucrats about kinds of people emerge for regulating people acting under these words: citizenship (in) law.

Notice that we have used citizenship (in) law twice in these dynamic enactments. As we shall see below, citizenship (in) law involves two instances. There are *laws of citizenship*, which produce the words for partitioning, individuating, and aggregating peoples, and *citizenship laws* that regulate and govern peoples as named. We will further elaborate on this distinction later, but for now it is important to emphasise that laws of citizenship often articulate, allocate, and distribute rights and obligations and name kinds of people to which they apply; citizenship laws regulate these rights and obligations, often in distinct and separate fields of law such as family, labour, or criminal law. The laws of citizenship are often enacted as 'acts *on* citizenship', or nationality and citizenship laws are often embedded in diverse fields of law. This is one of the most essential elements of citizenship as an apparatus of government. This is because citizenship laws effectively conceal their logic relating to citizenship and present social, political, and legal transformations as specific struggles such as housing, sexuality, gender rather than broader struggles for citizenship as such.

Considering citizenship as an apparatus of government requires investigating how and when these five dynamic enactments are present and how various kinds of people are named. As we mentioned earlier, Deleuze identifies four lines that constitute an apparatus: visibility, utterance, force, and subjectivation. Each line is present in all the sites of citizenship as an apparatus of government, but each can be untangled (Deleuze [1989] 2006, 340). Hacking mentions various kinds of people who are traversed by these lines (2007, 285). He speaks, for example, about the avalanche of numbers in the nineteenth century on various categories of people: murderers, thieves, prostitutes, drunks, vagrants, the insane, the poor, and all sorts of deviants. Where did these people come from? Did they not exist before the nineteenth century in some form? Hacking says acts that people performed to get named existed historically (e.g., stealing, killing, drinking) but how those acts were used to name, count, and classify peoples are made up and change often. He says 'even national and provincial censuses amazingly show that the categories into which people fall change every ten years. Social and political change creates new categories of people, but the counting is no mere report of developments. It elaborately, often philanthropically, creates new ways for people to be' (2002, 100). The invented categories that Hacking mentions involve many different 'ways to be' such as those of sexuality, ethnicity, or race. Hacking, for example, says 'the homosexual and the heterosexual as kinds of persons (as ways to be persons, or as conditions of personhood) came into being only toward the end of the nineteenth century' (2002, 103). Historically there were sex acts between individuals, but such acts came under familiar and recognisable (sayable, visible, sensible) words only in the nineteenth century. And there is no guarantee that these words will live forever. So his significant claim 'is not that there was a kind of person who came increasingly to be recognized by [apparatuses of government], but rather that a kind of person came into being at the same time as the kind itself was being invented' (2002, 106).

To put it differently, it is not that a kind of people never existed before and came into being at a certain moment. Nor is it that a kind of people always existed and was named in a particular moment. Rather, at a certain moment in history people did not experience themselves in this particular way, they did not interact with other people in this way, and were not treated by knowledge, institutions, authorities under this description. So, making up people as citizen subjects requires dynamic enactments. Understanding how peoples are partitioned (e.g., idle versus productive), individuated (e.g., vagrant, deviant, thief, prostitute), and aggregated (e.g., citizen, stranger, outsider, alien) is not possible without investigating these dynamic enactments.

When Hacking talks about 'making up people' he means kinds of people. And these are typically the scope of citizenship laws. There are kinds of people created such as blacks, flaneurs, indigenous, men, migrants, murderers, queers, refugees, teenagers, terrorists, and women and many others that constitute 'parts' of a 'whole'. Yet these kinds of people as 'parts' are unimaginable unless there are kinds of people who have been constituted as a 'whole' by citizenship as an apparatus of government. To put it differently, individuation and aggregating peoples is not possible without partitioning them. A people can be named only when a line between peoples (parts) and *the* people (whole) is created by apparatuses of government. The people as a whole involves a more complicated history than Hacking considers, as it involves the relation between the whole and its parts. This is because the dynamic enactment between words and things that Hacking addresses involves apparatus, and there are plays of domination and emancipation in the enactment between words and things. The words 'black' or 'queer' are not only descriptions under which a people will act but are also asymmetrical signifiers under which a people will be acted upon – these kinds will be subjects of government as citizens or noncitizens. Moreover, it is one thing to see how the name homosexual has come about, it is another to understand how its difference was created by naming people as heterosexuals, thereby first individuating and then aggregating kinds of people into the people as a whole. The question that we must address is not only the invention of kinds of people but also the invention of *the* people. To put it differently, the question 'what is a people?' inevitably leads to the question 'what is *the* people?' This is the importance of the distinction we maintain above between the laws of citizenship (that constitute the people as a whole) and citizenship laws that regulate kinds of people that are part of the body.

The history of citizenship as an apparatus of government provides numerous examples of this process of partition, individuation, and aggregation. This history develops from the ancient Greek *demos* to Roman *plebeians* to medieval Italian *popolo* (Canovan 2005). This is a history of struggles between those who constitute themselves as claimants of rights against dominant classes – against which and through which they are defined – often as patricians or aristocrats. The two histories (demos, plebs, and popolo) and the people are often thought separately. There is political thinking on demos, plebs, and popolo, and there is political thinking on the people as such often described as 'we, the people'. Yet, the fracture between the people as a whole and its partitions and aggregations (peoples), let alone how this fracture assembles citizenship as an apparatus of government, is our interest here. The respectable, unified, and virtuous stories of the people as a whole are often narrated against the unruly mob and herd, or rebellious and ungovernable, or inadequate and incapable. Agamben is right to designate this fracture as essential to political thinking. Agamben says that 'any interpretation of the political meaning of the term people ought to start from the peculiar fact that in modern European languages this term always also indicates the poor, the underprivileged, and the excluded' ([1996] 2000, 29). This is because 'the same term names the constitutive [citizen] subject as well as the class that is excluded – de facto, if not de jure – from politics' (29).

Agamben notes that 'people' is associated with the excluded because '... the term became the equivalent for misfortune and unhappiness ...' (30). Agamben notes, however, that from the beginning of political thinking about 'people' there is an ambiguity about whether it means the constitutive dominant or the dominated or both. For Agamben then 'such a widespread and constant semantic ambiguity cannot be accidental: it surely reflects an ambiguity inherent in the nature and function of the concept of people in Western politics' (31). For Agamben 'the constitution of the human species into a body politic comes into being through a fundamental split and that in the concept of people we can easily recognize the conceptual pair identified earlier as the defining category of the original political structure' (31–32) and this involves naked life (*peoples*) and political life (*the people*).

Agamben concludes that '*The concept of people always already contains within itself the fundamental biopolitical fracture. It is what cannot be included in the whole of which it is a part as well as what cannot belong to the whole in which it is always already included'* (32, emphasis original). Thus, 'if this is the case – if the concept of people necessarily contains within itself the fundamental biopolitical fracture – it is possible to read anew some decisive pages of the history of our century' (33). For Agamben when '… sovereignty is entrusted solely to the people, the *people* become an embarrassing presence, and poverty and exclusion appear for the first time as an intolerable scandal in every sense' (32). We can say that the scandal of citizenship arises when the people as a whole attempt to aggregate peoples as its parts and yet peoples still remain as individuated by class, race, gender, and other names.

There has been much debate about what Agamben calls the biopolitical fracture between the people as a whole and peoples, which we named as a fracture between the people as a whole and peoples as its parts. Whether this fracture can be defined as between a naked life (*zoē*) and political life (*bios*) is outside our discussion. As we shall see this fracture produces more refined names than a fracture between bare life and political life since citizenship as an apparatus of government institutes a hierarchy between the people as a whole and its parts (peoples). We can focus on this problem with Jacques Rancière ([1995] 1998) and Ernesto Laclau (2005) who also identify this fracture. For both scholars the fracture between the people as a whole and peoples as its parts is constitutive of politics and its apparatuses.

For Rancière, politics arises from a scandal. Rancière uses a specific language of the whole and its parts to describe this scandal. The 'whole' is a polity and 'parts' are its constitutive elements. This language enables Rancière to avoid more established sociological and anthropological categories such as 'classes' and 'social groups' since these categories are already given names that decide the distribution of parts that constitute the whole. For Rancière, what gives rise to politics is the struggle over what counts as parts. He says dominant interpretations of ancient politics read this politics as arising from an already constituted polity and its already existing conflicts; however, he says, it is actually the other way around. A polity is founded on politics and counting the parts constitutes it. Politics arises from the counting of parts; and it is struggles over what counts that constitute a polity.

For Rancière, there are two ways of counting: arithmetic and geometric. An arithmetic counting assumes that all is accounted for (hence always a false count); a geometric counting counts those parts that have no part. When counting is arithmetic (as in what is counted), it accounts for what is given; when it is geometric (as in what counts), it accounts for what is not given. Yet, and this is crucial, counts are always false counts as they fall short of considering of what actually counts. Politics arises from this paradox of being unable to and yet needing to count parts (Rancière [1995] 1998, 6). The scandal arises from those who have no part actually being enabled to make themselves count (9). What is scandalous about parts making themselves count is that the parts that have no part identify themselves as being the whole of the political body. It is this audacious identification that is the scandal of politics. This is, for example, the historical significance of demos in Athenian politics. The claim of demes is not only to make themselves count but also to constitute itself as the whole. So then the language of those who have no part is not about an essential struggle between the rich and the poor, between this and that class, or between this and that social group – although all these can be mapped onto it. Politics is not an opposition between the rich and the poor, but it is the rupture of an order of domination by the emancipation of a part of those who have no part (11).

What accomplishes the partition of the people into parts and aggregates these parts into a whole are demands or claims for equality and wrong. The struggles of those who have no part to institute themselves as a part is based on their claims to equality and their declaration of wrong. The claim against inequality is necessary for the declaration of wrong and that declaration is impossible without the assumption of equality of speech and capacity, an equal part in dispute. If indeed 'politics exists wherever the count of parts and parties of society is disturbed by the inscription of a part of those who have no part' it begins when the equality of anyone and everyone is inscribed in the liberty of the people (Rancière [1995] 1998, 123). And 'this liberty of the people is an empty property, an improper property through which those who are nothing purport that their group is identical to the whole of the community' (123–4). So, emancipation of a people as a claim is simultaneously the origins of politics and its scandal.

What is the people as a whole that the people want to be a part of? Sometimes 'the people' simply means any people. Other times it means the people as a whole. Like Agamben, Rancière thinks that this double embodiment is a fundamental fracture: it is both the name of a whole of the people as a polity and the name of a part of that polity. The gap between these two names of the people becomes the site of a struggle (Rancière [1992] 1995, 97). While ancient politics understood this gap, says Rancière, modern politics cannot tolerate it. Modern politics cannot accept that the people simultaneously can be both sovereign and not sovereign, whole and part (99).

Although not concerned with the ancient origins of modern politics, Laclau is closer to Rancière when identifying the fundamental fracture that gives rise to politics. At the centre of his argument is the category of 'demands' articulated by the dominated to the dominant. They articulate an exclusion or deprivation as their grievance, and it is such demands that constitute a people (Laclau 2005, 123). As with Rancière then the people and its parts are not already given categories, but they arise with and from politics. This recognises that there is a constitutive asymmetry between a polity understood as a whole (the *populus*) and the dominated as its part (the plebs). For Laclau, as for Rancière, it is crucial that the plebs identify themselves with the *populus* as the polity as a whole (Laclau 2005, 224). Thus, as in Rancière, the plebs function both as part of a whole and a part that is the whole (Laclau 2005, 225). The logic of hegemony that arises from this tension between the people as a whole and peoples as its parts implies that the whole is 'contaminated' by the part and the part contains the whole. The analytical distinction between the universal (the people as a whole) and the particular (peoples as its parts) as though they are mutually exclusive opposites belies the logic of hegemony (Laclau 2005, 226). The ambiguity of 'the people' both as the *populus* and the plebs is not a logical contradiction but expresses the logic of hegemony. Laclau differs from Rancière. For Rancière assumes that the constitution of the part that has no part will always invoke a politics of emancipation. By contrast, Laclau does not think that this can be determined theoretically (246). Laclau also insists on limits of theoretical analysis and the necessity of sociological investigation of the ways in which the logic of hegemony constitutes a people (248).

Agamben, Rancière and Laclau are necessary for understanding the fracture between the people as a whole (we, the people) and parts (peoples), how this partition, individuation, and aggregation is performed and how it creates the citizen subject as its indivisible part requires a concept of citizenship as an apparatus of government. What is required is to articulate how politics inevitably or not involves the making up of the people either as a whole or as parts and how the relationship between domination and emancipation plays out. If, as Rancière says, there is no politics beyond and outside this configuration of the whole and its parts and that 'there is only the order of domination or the disorder of revolt' then it necessarily raises the question of how citizenship as an apparatus of government functions ([1995] 1998, 12). If we follow Agamben, Rancière, and Laclau, the whole (the people) and its parts (peoples) are implicated in each other. How can we investigate citizenship as an apparatus of government that creates the people as a whole and its parts? All understand politics as rupture in a given order. In particular, Laclau says that the creation of a people involves an act of institution and as an act it does not derive its force 'from any logic already operating within the preceding situation' and that 'what is crucial for the emergence of "the people" as a new historical actor is that the unification of plurality of demands in a new configuration is constitutive and not derivative' (2005, 228). For Laclau the institution of the people as a whole 'constitutes an *act* in the strict sense, for it does not have its source in anything external to itself' (228). We shall return to acts and rupture later, but for now, let us outline how we can investigate the fractures of citizenship as an apparatus of government and how it assembles the apparatus together.

Although Agamben, Rancière, and Laclau raise the question of how the people as a whole and peoples as its parts are constituted together, it is Hacking who shows how a people comes to be. Our question is how citizenship as an apparatus of government constitutes the people as a whole and its parts by partitioning, individuating, and aggregating peoples and by performing both domination and emancipation across dynamic enactments. We mentioned earlier that we will outline a modified approach inspired by Hacking's outline of how a people comes to be across four sites of enactment of citizenship. To capture the distinct but overlapping logics of these sites, we shall use the convention (in) to draw attention to the making of the citizen partitioned by a fracture between the people as a whole and its parts. If, for example, *laws of citizenship* concerns legislation about citizenship as such that constitutes the people as a whole, there are also *citizenship laws* that shape citizenship: labour laws, healthcare laws, family laws, tax laws, or housing laws that are not citizenship laws as such but shape rights enjoyed by or denied to citizens and noncitizens. The phrase 'citizenship (in) law' captures both laws of citizenship and citizenship laws.

Likewise, citizenship (in) theory captures both *political thinking* that produces knowledge about how citizenship ought to function by comparing current practices against its apparatus and *thinking politically* which emerges out of struggles to control or resignify citizenship as an apparatus of government. While both may produce, provoke, and invoke an imaginary of the whole, their practical situatedness means that they perform distinct functions.

And, similarly, there are also citizenship practices where citizens are interpellated into becoming citizens with rights and obligations such as taxation, involuntary or military or jury duties, political duties (voting, office holding), unemployment and retirement benefits and so on. There are, however, citizenship practices that are not specifically named but nonetheless enable citizens and noncitizens to practise citizenship by getting involved in diverse activities from protesting, assembling, and gathering to volunteering. While dominating citizenship practices specifically interpellate people into an apparatus of the people (nation, state, society), emancipatory citizenship practices interpellate diverse peoples as its parts in struggle with or against the apparatus. Citizenship (in) practice captures these entangled modes but untangles them.

Finally, citizenship (in) acts captures both juridical acts (acts *on* citizenship) that control who can act as citizens and those acts that rupture these borders and orders (acts *of* citizenship). Their rupture has significant effects on the ways in which the imaginary of the people as a whole is instituted and the principles of partition, individuation, and aggregation of its peoples into the people as a whole. Acts on citizenship are attempts to capture citizenship as an apparatus of government with all its details, and they are always revised. Whether they are embedded in the constitution or a series of supplements, acts on citizenship are continuous attempts to institute the imaginary of the people as whole by aggregating while simultaneously partitioning and individuating its peoples.

The underlying logic of using (in) for these sites is that while some struggles over citizenship occur explicitly for or under the name 'citizenship' others occur under different names, often associated with specific rights over which there are social struggles such as reproductive rights or disability rights. Thus, using (in) signals that investigating citizenship both across and within these sites is necessary to reveal how it is assembled or brought into being as an apparatus of government. How do we go about investigating the assembling of citizenship as an apparatus of government which aggregates and individuates peoples as parts into the people as a whole and the struggles over domination and emancipation that it provokes?

Citizenship (in) law

If citizenship is an apparatus by which governments create the appropriate administrative arrangements for partitioning peoples, individuating groups, and aggregating individuals as citizen subjects of government, the primary means by which partition and aggregation occur is through what we call the laws of citizenship. As mentioned above, the distinction we make here between the laws of citizenship and citizenship laws is necessary for understanding citizenship as an apparatus of government. The laws of citizenship partition people primarily into *jus sanguinis* (whereby a child inherits citizenship via a parent), *jus soli* (whereby a child inherits citizenship via birthplace), or *jus domicili* (whereby an adult acquires citizenship by naturalisation in a state other than that of their birth) and sets out laws of acquisition and deprivation. The laws of citizenship codify the rights and obligations of citizens as the people as a whole and its parts are defined.

The laws of citizenship simultaneously create both citizen and noncitizen categories and specify powers to act through these categories across numerous citizenship laws. Citizenship (in) law embodies and reveals these two different logics. The laws of citizenship are often laws that outline categories of persons and legal capabilities or incapabilities. The laws of citizenship are laws that govern the relation between citizens (and noncitizens) and the polity. The laws of citizenship are abstract because they outline categories of persons and their rights and obligations. The laws of citizenship create borders and orders.

By contrast, governing citizens and noncitizens through citizenship laws generates concrete legal or illegal conduct because, rather than creating categories of people, they outline the boundaries between legal and illegal for each category of people and their subcategories. Labour laws concerning age discrimination, bullying and harassment, disability, race, religion, sexuality or gender discrimination, dismissal and employee grievances, employment contracts, equal pay, holiday pay, minimum wage, parental leave, redundancy, and working hours are examples of a field of law that embodies rights that emerge out of citizenship without naming it. Diverse fields of law such as on crime, economy, education, energy, environment, family, finance, health, housing, migration, military, security, and taxation laws specify rights and obligations of citizens and noncitizens and outline borders and orders of conduct.

Once individuated into these diverse fields, citizenship laws no longer appear as citizenship as such at all but as specific fields of application. Moreover, their relations with each other often remain concealed. Therein lies the logic of domination: by individuating and then aggregating, classifying, and categorising, citizenship effectively conceals itself from citizens as an apparatus of government. This immense apparatus is never transparent to citizens in their relations with each other and with the polities to which they belong. While a part of the people as a whole, people effectively experience citizenship alone, isolated, and atomised. While interpellated to imagine themselves as the people as a whole, citizens nonetheless experience this only as isolated and individuated people as subjects of law.

With the development of international law, human rights law, and transnational conventions especially in the last 75 years, citizenship (in) law is not contained or containable only within sovereign polities. Citizenship (in) law draws on various repertoires of making rights claims through national, international, transnational, and human rights and creates complex assemblages of citizenship. Enacting laws of citizenship and citizenship laws creates overlapping and conflicting legitimacy and authority. Reiner Bauböck (2010) suggests studying citizenship as constellations signifying the overlapping authority, legitimacy, and legality of citizenship. These overlaps and conflicts create possibilities for citation, resignification, repetition, and rupture of citizenship (in) law. To distinguish between laws of citizenship and citizenship laws enables us to observe how citizenship is enacted not only in laws of citizenship where it is named but also in citizenship laws where citizenship is not named but present.

Although we will discuss Hannah Arendt later, we will mention our distinction between laws of citizenship and citizenship laws with respect to her conception of citizenship as the right to have rights. For Arendt the right to have rights is a fundamental right because it enables citizens to articulate and struggle for non-fundamental rights. She considers the citizen as a fundamental subjectivity to develop and maintain ourselves as citizen subjects making rights claims. At first this appears similar to the distinction we make between laws of citizenship and citizenship laws. Yet Arendt considers a fracture between the people as a whole (state) and peoples as its parts (nations) as given, where peoples may or may not be part of the body, but they may still have rights. For Arendt the problem is when any of its parts (nations) constitutes itself as the people as a whole (state). This fracture between laws of citizenship (that constitute a body of citizens) and citizenship laws (that regulate their conduct) is not constative but performative: the right to act as a citizen can come from outside the authority of a given polity.

Citizenship (in) theory

We saw earlier with Charles Tilly (1997). that a striking aspect of citizenship is that it forces people into normative positions – for or against citizenship. From our perspective these positions are performative: people often do something with citizenship as an apparatus of government.

The problem becomes intractable if we conflate two modes of performativity: between political thinking and thinking politically in citizenship (in) theory and citizenship (in) theory and citizenship (in) practice. When we are analysing an utterance on citizenship, drawing on Freeden (2013), we distinguish between political thinking where analytical interpretation is the objective and thinking politically where interventions are objectives. When an utterance of citizenship (in) theory is analysed, we must also not assume that citizenship (in) practice works as described by the utterance. The ideas, ideals, interpretations, explanations, contentions about what citizenship is (or ought to be) produce citizenship (in) theory, either as political thinking or thinking politically, and neither quite coincides with citizenship (in) practice. Although citizenship (in) theory, either as political thinking or thinking politically, attempts to describe citizenship (in) practice, it still performs citizenship but not as it imagines, as each performs a different role in interpellating people into being citizens. Making matters more complicated, the study of citizenship as such is quite recent and the authors who have been cited, repeated, and resignified in citizenship (in) theory for 2,500 years have performed in both modes of political thinking and thinking politically and often crossed between the two modes. Just consider the following illustrious but still incredibly short list: Solon (630–560 BCE), Aristotle (384–322 BCE), Cicero (106–43 BCE), Tacitus (56–120), Bartolus de Saxoferrato (1313–1357), Baldus de Ubaldis (1327–1400), Niccolò Machiavelli (1469–1527), Jean Bodin (1530–1596), Thomas Hobbes (1588–1679), John Locke (1632–1704), Montesquieu (1689–1755), Jean-Jacques Rousseau (1712–1778), John S. Mill (1806–1873). The list includes statesmen, jurists, poets, generals, lawyers, and scholars, some of whom often crossed between the two modes. While it is somehow assumed that these authors mirror citizenship (in) practice or citizenship (in) law, it is always difficult to distinguish between different author-functions through which they perform their citizenship. Authorship about citizenship (in) theory only partially overlaps with citizenship (in) law and citizenship (in) practice and a gap opens, which remains as concealed as ever.

Given this complexity, historical studies of citizenship that primarily focus on citizenship (in) theory rarely recognise or accept that citizenship (in) theory may have been radically different from citizenship (in) practice or citizenship (in) law, or that it may have been performed in political thinking or thinking politically modes. Scholars such as Derek Heater (1990), Andreas Fahrmeir (2008), J.G.A. Pocock (1992), and Peter Riesenberg (1992) have written influential histories of political thinking about citizenship, but without placing these performative utterances within diverse practices of thinking politically, these accounts tend to conceal their author-functions. Rousseau or Hobbes were performative authors whose political thinking was attuned (and perhaps intended) to do something with citizenship as an apparatus of government embodied in thinking politically about citizenship. To put it differently, when citizenship is assembled as an apparatus of government through performative utterances, either in political thinking or thinking politically, without giving an account of the placement of the utterances in the apparatus and the fractures through which they author-function, their object – citizenship – appears as a (historically and geographically) stable and independent concept. It has become especially customary to emplace utterances on citizenship (without distinguishing their modes of utterance) in the last 200 hundred years into various categories such as liberal, republican, and communitarian as either ideologies or philosophies. This often assumes that these utterances are descriptions of citizenship (in) practice when they were being produced of, in, and by doing something with citizenship as an apparatus of government. It is difficult to avoid the conclusion that these only serve to conceal the apparatus of citizenship.

Given this long history, the articulations of citizenship (in) theory within universities is an even more recent development (Kymlicka and Wayne 1994). Until about 100 years ago the development of citizenship (in) theory in sociology, politics, anthropology, and geography, most scholars were reflecting on questions of governing a polity (e.g., city, state, empire, league, federation) and the rights and obligations of its constituent peoples. If we take the studies of Max Weber ([1921] 1978; 1927a) on the origins of polities, cities, and capitalism, the influential work of T.H. Marshall ([1949] 1996) on class and citizenship, and the significant work of Bryan Turner (1986) on citizenship and capitalism as three significant moments in the development of the study of citizenship in universities, we can make two observations. All three see citizenship from the perspective of the state. Yet all three also revolutionise the study of citizenship by transgressing the boundaries between constative and performative. Each does this differently. Weber invests in citizenship as a political possibility by showing how citizenship functions. Marshall insists that only citizenship especially social citizenship can provide a modicum of security and welfare to maintain a democratic state. And Turner shows that the increasing demands of social movements for transforming citizenship by expanding rights cultivates a just order and maintains a democratic state.

With the development of the study of citizenship in the last 40 years since Weber, Marshall, and Turner, and especially with the emergence of citizenship studies as a field in the last 25 years, we have reached a new juncture. For reasons that we have already mentioned in this book, it became impossible to maintain that citizenship remains only within polities called states or nations. City, regional, transnational, and inter-national pressures on citizenship as an apparatus of government traverse polities. It has also become impossible to maintain the legitimacy of the existing hierarchical partitioning of peoples into various groups that held a nation or state together. The apparatuses partitioning, individuating, and aggregating peoples have been challenged, refused, resisted, resigni-fied, subverted, and brought into question. Citizenship as an apparatus of government is being taken apart and reassembled. To put it differently, the division between ancient and modern, colonial, and postcolonial, nomadic and sedentary, human and nonhuman, and between disembodied and embodied technologies in citizenship as an apparatus of government have been breached.

Today as academics participate in citizenship (in) theory by developing theoretical, analytical, and methodological tools with which to understand and teach citizenship (in) law, citizenship (in) practice, and citizenship (in) acts there is much disagreement on who are the subjects of citizenship. The precise articulations of citizenship in movement, technology, coloniality, sovereignty, and planetarity generate immense tensions between and amongst citizenship (in) law, (in) theory, (in) practice, and (in) acts. This is because of the instability arising from the breaches in borders and orders that both sustain and arise from citizenship as an apparatus of government. This instability is articulated by diverse demands for abolishing borders and orders and even citizenship as an apparatus of government. But instability is not necessarily an undesirable development. They are potentially revolutionary developments, and we will return to this aspect of citizenship at the end of this book.

Citizenship (in) theory is not only performed by scholars. Citizenship (in) theory includes statements and utterances by citizens and noncitizens as activists, artists, authorities, bureaucrats, entrepreneurs, intellectuals, journalists, politicians, and professionals who enact citizenship in multiple ways. Each author, either in struggle or solidarity with another, makes claims about rights and obligations, affinities and loyalties, justices and injustices, grievances, and objections and is interpellated to citizenship as an apparatus of government. As in the difference between laws of citizenship and citizenship laws these claims are about citizenship as such or its diverse fields of application.

More provocatively citizenship (in) theory also includes animals, forests, lakes, mountains, planets, plants, rivers, robots, seas, and volcanoes. We are becoming increasingly attuned to hearing nonhuman citizens and noncitizens and their utterances in citizenship (in) theory. We are witnessing the interpellation of nonhuman actants into citizenship as an apparatus of government. Ecological activists or animal activists are opening the possibilities of acting together with nonhuman actants.

Each category follows its logics of production. Citizenship (in) theory is neither reducible to nor can exhaust citizenship (in) law or citizenship (in) practice. This an important aspect of the assemblage of citizenship as an apparatus of government. How citizenship is performed through tensions amongst and between citizenship (in) law, (in) practice, and (in) acts determines whether, as an apparatus of government, it functions for domination or emancipation.

Citizenship (in) practice

Citizenship (in) law and citizenship (in) practice have overlapping but distinct logics. The latter does not simply 'follow' the former. Nor does the former simply 'respond' to the latter. People take up their citizenship (in) practice and perform rights and obligations in diverse and complicated ways, mixing and matching different rights, making claims to new ones, resisting the disappearance of others, and, in the process, traversing borders and orders. Often people do not concern themselves with the sources of their rights in making claims or how citizenship (in) law (either as laws of citizenship or citizenship laws) specifies their powers to act. As we have seen, citizenship (in) theory also has distinct but overlapping logics with citizenship (in) law; we will now see that citizenship (in) practice also has distinct and overlapping logics. When Pierre Bourdieu ([1980] 1990, 86) insists that 'practice has a logic which is not that of the logician. This has to be acknowledged in order to avoid asking of it more logic than it can give, thereby condemning oneself either to wring incoherences out of it or to thrust a forced coherence upon it', he is referring to these distinct logics. Unlike Bourdieu, however, we have to recognise that often the logic of the logician is not more coherent than the logic of the practitioner either. It is therefore essential that we distinguish logics of political thinking and thinkingly politically separately in citizenship (in) law, citizenship (in) practice, and then citizenship (in) theory, bearing in mind that the sequence in which we are discussing them is nonetheless arbitrary.

When people are performing citizenship (in) practice, mixing and matching rights, they often draw on laws of citizenship, but they simultaneously shape citizenship laws. The struggles against the colour line (racialisation) illustrates this. When people struggle against the domination of black and brown people – categories that were instituted by citizenship (in) law – the object of their demands and their claims is not citizenship laws as such alone but also laws of citizenship in the workplace, elections, neighbourhood, school, entertainment, or sports that raises the question of why black and brown people are marginalised, discriminated, dispossessed, or dominated. How are the possibilities and potentialities of a people who are trapped into racial categories oppressed?

Through various anti-racist practices when people amend citizenship laws (e.g., labour laws, election laws, housing laws, education laws, advertising laws), they also begin to reveal a fundamental question: why are black and brown people or indigenous people dispossessed by the laws of citizenship? So, what begins as specific and concrete questions articulating into claims to citizenship laws, gradually and sometimes rapidly articulates into fundamental questions of inclusion, exclusion, justice, and equality in laws of citizenship and transforms citizenship as an apparatus of government that partitions peoples as black and white, defines the peoples as a whole as white, individuates peoples by ascriptive designations, and aggregates them as categories.

We see the same logic when citizenship as an apparatus of government constitutes a polity along majority versus minority lines. When any polity partitions peoples into ethnic, religious, or language groups, defines the people as a whole by designating one group as the people, individuates them with ascriptions, and aggregates them into majorities and minorities, citizenship as an apparatus of government institutionalises these lines and fractures.

With recent historical experience, we can extend the struggles against racism to include the struggles of women, indigenous peoples, queer peoples, people with so-called disabilities, where making many rights claims in specific and citizenship laws began fundamentally altering laws of citizenship and raising a question about how these categories of persons were created and were dominated by hegemonic categories of persons such as Western, white, male, heterosexual, secular, and able-bodied.

We must also observe that these gaps between citizenship (in) law and citizenship (in) practice create possibilities. We cannot understand citizenship (in) law without documenting how it is embodied, observed, enforced, transgressed, subverted, or even perverted as citizenship (in) practice.

There are immense varieties of citizenship (in) practice. It ranges from routine practices such as voting to active practices such as serving on juries, to activist practices such as protests, assembly, campaigning, lobbying, and demonstrating. As we discussed earlier, these practices can engage both laws of citizenship and citizenship laws in multiple fields of law. Although Charles Tilly (2008) does not necessarily see it as citizenship (in) practice, his enumeration of contentious performances is an illustration of how widespread they are.

Nonetheless, we can broadly distinguish between dominating and emancipating citizenship practices. It is this fold that the convention citizenship (in) practice aims to capture. We have given above examples of emancipatory citizenship practices that struggle against the dominant practices of citizenship as an apparatus of government partitioning, individuating, and aggregating peoples into the people as a whole with all the injustices and often violences that this implies. The partitioning, individuating, and aggregating of peoples into the people as a whole is never complete, stable, or uncontested. Each polity therefore expends immense energy and force to maintain the citizen subject as its most indivisible part as obedient, submissive, and disciplined. In fact, it is this function of citizenship as an apparatus of government that integrates with other apparatuses of government such as security, health, education, and economy to produce the citizen subject. We do not have space in this book to study in detail how this integration between citizenship (in) practice and various apparatuses of government happens through citizenship (in) law (both laws of citizenship and citizenship laws). The parts of citizenship as an apparatus of government below may suffice to illustrate how this integration happens.

Consider first how laws of citizenship partition peoples into citizens and noncitizens. This partitioning invokes a massive and costly security apparatus that aims to control the territory of the polity by organising, controlling, and building borders where this partitioning is put into effect. An external security apparatus creates borders ranging from conventional walls, fences, perimeters, and checkpoints to biometric, virtual, and shifting borders with sophisticated surveillance technologies. As Todd Miller (2019) documents, the territory of a polity does not only include contiguous and contained spaces but extraterritorial zones, corridors, frequencies, and other technologies of partitioning peoples and spaces simultaneously. Maintaining these borders and partitioning people gives rise to elaborate deportation, detention, offshore and onshore processing, incarceration, and migration regimes, producing a tentacular apparatus of governing movements of peoples by the dominant polities especially (Mountz 2011).

Conversely, the partitioning of peoples into citizens (the people as a whole) and noncitizens (peoples) also provokes an internal security apparatus in integration with financial, labour, crime, health, and education apparatuses to partition, individuate, and aggregate peoples. Citizens become partitioned into taxpaying (or not), employed (or not), lawful (or not), healthy (or not), and educated (or not) ascriptions where they experience their citizenship differently. Similarly, noncitizens become further individuated into migrants, refugees, aliens, foreigners, residents, and so on. Being a citizen subject caught in this apparatus of government means a constant struggle over crossing multiples lines between partitions, individuations, and aggregations.

Consider then how laws of citizenship on both acquisition and deprivation (or revocation) of citizenship individuates, aggregates, or rejects peoples in the people as a whole (Shaw 2020). Of those partitioned and aggregated into the people as a whole and those who will be either rejected or accepted into the polity, each polity expends considerable force and energy to enact citizenship laws on acquisition and deprivation or revocation of citizenship (Troy 2019). Both citizenship laws constitute the backbone of citizenship as an apparatus of government as this is where fractures of citizenship are inscribed on the bodies of citizens. Citizenship acquisition laws often prescribe both ethical and political utterances as legal principles to determine the eligibility, protocol, process, and requirements for citizenship acquisition. The acquisition has been conventionally consummated during citizenship ceremonies involving the oath as an act of citizenship inaugurating the citizen subject into the polity.

Movements against this tentacular apparatus of government, which certainly involves citizenship as an apparatus of government, force regimes to open borders and question legal and political reasons for partitioning peoples (Walia 2021; Tazzioli 2020). As we shall see both below and later, these movements are the pioneer movements to make citizenship as an apparatus of government sensible and intelligible.

These two parts of the apparatus illustrate how they combine with other apparatuses to control the composition of the body of citizens as the people as a whole by integrating or rendering noncitizens as migrants, refugees, or foreigners. The magic performed by these parts is that both citizens and noncitizens will feel the absence or lack of citizenship as obligations: those accepted will become citizen subjects as subjects of and subjects to power and will be interpellated to perform their obligations as citizens and enjoy their rights, and those rejected will continue to find ways to cross its lines. This of course may be interrupted when it becomes sensible and intelligible that the body of citizens one is absorbed by is as fractured as the body of noncitizens that is rejected. That may become the conditions of possibility of performing acts of citizenship.

Citizenship (in) acts

Acts of citizenship signifies a performative politics of citizenship: in and by making rights claims, people constitute themselves as citizens, often against any convention that may yet exist to authorise their act (Zivi 2012). To say that citizenship is performed in acts may be stating the obvious. As we have seen in our discussion of citizenship (in) law, laws of citizenship are often enacted as acts on citizenship by legislative bodies. Often, citizenship (in) law comes into being through acts on citizenship, which we called laws of citizenship. Citizenship is also enacted through citizenship laws, diverse fields of law where citizenship is not the object of legislation but has influence on it. We cited labour, family, migration, and health laws as examples of laws of citizenship. There are fundamental differences between acts on citizenship (either in laws of citizenship law or citizenship laws) and acts of citizenship that disrupt the existing laws or practices. To distinguish between the two modes of performing citizenship, we call the former acts *on* citizenship and the latter acts *of* citizenship. We have discussed acts on citizenship in relation to both citizenship (in) law and citizenship (in) practice. Our focus here is acts of citizenship as a constitutive part of citizenship as an apparatus of government where its fractures are rendered sensible and intelligible. To put it differently, it is acts of citizenship that rupture the assemblage of citizenship as an apparatus of government. We become aware of fractures of citizenship – movement, technology, coloniality, sovereignty, and planetarity – because acts of citizenship reveal and expose them. We will discuss acts of citizenship in three separate occasions in this book. Below we will focus on technical aspects through performativity. In Chapter 3, we have a more detailed discussion about making rights claims as the constitutive aspects of acts of citizenship. And, in Chapter 4, we have yet another discussion of the relation between acts of citizenship, revolts, and indeed revolutions.

Acts have a performative meaning to signify a deed or an action. Through such deeds collectives enact their political subjectivity and constitute themselves as claimants of rights. These acts can be as diverse as singing, dramatising, occupying, contesting, mocking, striking, satirising, and many more acts through which people make claims to rights – such as residence, work, or asylum – that they do not have, campaign for a right that they have lost (such as the right to social care or education), or protest a right accorded to others and that should not exist, as in the case of corporate offshore tax havens.

What is the difference between the speaking subject and the citizen subject? How do acts bring citizen subjects into being? To understand language as social activity rather than only as means of communication is to investigate how people do things with words in ordinary language. Of course, J.L Austin made an immense contribution to our understanding of the relationship between words and things. How people do things with words is much more creative and inventive than a conception of speaking subjects following rules. If we work with the idea of speaking subjects following rules, we fail to recognise the practical creativity and inventiveness of people in action *with* language.

Although a speech act for Austin (1962) often involves doing things with words, he is critical of the dominant view that treats a speech act as a description. Austin designates this descriptive element of speech acts as constatives. When we use statements such as 'I am typing', we are describing what we are doing. It is a constative speech act. It describes a state of affairs; it makes a truth claim; and it can be verified or falsified. As a constative speech act, it is a statement that signifies a meaning. By contrast, when a statement either warns about something or urges someone to do something, it moves from being a statement to being an utterance. It accomplishes an act by its *force*. Austin says that there are many verbs in the English language that can be classified according to these effects of meaning and force. Austin uses three connectives to classify speech acts: 'of', 'in', and 'by'. For 'of', Austin says: the act *of* saying something is a locutionary act. This is a speech act whose *meaning* calls forth a true versus false distinction and requires verification or falsification. The effect or consequence of a locutionary act – a constative – is to produce or fail to produce a meaningful description of a state of affairs. For 'in', as *in* saying something we may be doing something, Austin says it produces an illocutionary act. This is a speech act whose *force* creates a *potential* effect in a state of affairs that it seeks to describe. What it invokes is not verification or falsification but whether there is an uptake. To put it another way, whether an utterance is successful (felicitous) or unsuccessful (infelicitous) is determined by its force. As Shoshana Felman writes, 'since ... to speak is to act, performative utterances, inasmuch as they produce actions, and constitute operations, cannot be logically true or false, but only successful or unsuccessful, "felicitous" or "infelicitous"' ([1980] 2003, 115). For example, in saying, 'I am writing my will', I am indicating that I am bequeathing. Although my speech act places me under an obligation, I have not done anything yet. In saying something, I have brought forth – performative – conditions for something to happen. Finally, doing something *by* saying something is a perlocutionary act (Austin 1962). This is a speech act that must have an effect to be actualised. Like an illocutionary act, a perlocutionary act invokes an evaluation along felicitous or infelicitous lines rather than true or false. By saying that 'I am typing gibberish' (when you are anticipating otherwise), I may have annoyed you. (Perhaps I am under coercion to give a false statement.) By saying something, I have accomplished something. Thus, 'of' saying something has *meaning* (locutionary acts), whereas 'in' or 'by' saying something has *force* (illocutionary and perlocutionary acts).

The distinctions between meaning and force, between statement and utterance, and between constative and performative are key to understanding how speech acts are different from speech that describes. Austin gives examples of illocutionary acts, such as betting, bequeathing, warning, promising, and so on, and examples of the perlocutionary acts, such as persuading, annoying, thrilling, bullying, frightening, wounding, and so on (Cavell 1994, 81). By advancing the idea that speech is not only a description (constative) but also an act (performative), Austin ushers in a radically different way of thinking about not only speaking and writing but also doing things in or by speaking and writing.

Austin is as much interested in acts as words; or, more precisely, he is interested in acts that words perform. He observes that words will never be enough to accomplish an act, despite recognising that, without words at some stage, it is difficult to see how any act can be accomplished (Austin 1962, 12). So, first, although his examples are from speech, his interest is how words perform acts: 'to say something is to do something; or in which by saying or in saying something we are doing something' (Austin 1962, 87). Second, Austin recognises that nonverbal forms of speech such as bodily gestures and movements as well as visual and aural forms are always involved in the accomplishment of an act, especially in a perlocutionary act. So, Austin may not mention bodies much if at all, but bodies and their movements are implicit in speech that acts. To put it differently, speech or writing cannot act without bodies. Third, although all of Austin's examples are in the first person, he is not trapped by the speaking sovereign subject who is the master of their speech situation. On the contrary, as the illocutionary and perlocutionary acts indicate, in acting there are always infelicitous situations. As Cavell writes, Austin recognizes that acts will *also* occur 'unintentionally, unwillingly, involuntarily, insincerely, unthinkingly, inadvertently, heedlessly, carelessly, under duress, under the influence, out of contempt, out of pity, by mistake, by accident [and so on]' (1994, 148). To put it differently, Austin's concern with infelicitous is not a regret on his part but a recognition that speech does not only act, it can also fail to act or fail to act in the ways anticipated.

For Austin, investigating an act would require 'prolonged fieldwork', though he admits that is not what he is doing (1962, 148). But focusing on conventions of, in, and by which we act enables such investigations. For Austin, both the meaning of statements and force of utterances become possible by their appropriateness to the situation, which means an understanding of conventions governing a speech act situation. Citizenship (in) law, citizenship (in) practice and citizenship (in) theory are indeed such conventions. They embody norms, values, affects, laws, ideologies, and technologies. To judge the situation, the speaking subject must understand and perform in relation to the conventions governing what is sayable and doable in that place and time. The acting subject who speaks will have an understanding of not only the situation but also the appropriateness of what can and must be said and not said in that situation (Austin 1962, 8–9, 13, 26, 29, 34, 81–2).

For this reason, Bourdieu, drawing on Austin, insists that words themselves do not have inherent *meaning* or *force* but acquire them in social situations. For Bourdieu, speech acts are social acts and draw their force, illocutionary force if you like, not from linguistic apparatuses that govern them but from social apparatuses that make them possible. The things that render a subject capable of accomplishing an act are precisely the social apparatuses that guarantee its institution (Bourdieu 1991, 125–6). This is not to deny the power of words. But such power is nothing other than the delegated power of the speaker as a social subject (Bourdieu 1991, 107). This is, of course, another way of saying that a speech act is always a social act and a speaking subject a social subject. But do speaking subjects *merely* follow conventions (as Bourdieu seems to think)? The key issue in speech acts becomes whether, and if so to what extent, what is sayable and articulable follows or exceeds social conventions that govern a situation.

Austin is quite subtle on this point, but Judith Butler develops it in a creative way. For Austin, a general consideration is that although a speaking subject will rely on conventions to ascertain the meaning and force of their speech act, neither the meaning nor its force will ever be controllable by them. So, while a convention is a necessary condition of an act, almost equally it is also a necessary condition of its misfire – one of the 'ills that all action is heir to' (Austin 1962, 16, 25, 27, 105). That it requires conventions to accomplish an act and that it also provokes their transgression turns out to be a significant discovery of Austin. Butler makes use of this in theorising gender by drawing our attention to citation, repetition, and resignification of a convention and how these produce subjects of both submission *and* subversion. If a convention is to be cited to accomplish an act, a repetition of certain norms will be necessary. Yet each repetition will bring new circumstances to bear on the act, so much so that it is a resignification – a new deployment of a convention (Butler 1990, 173, 177–9; 2004, 218–24). But Austin reserves the transgression, or subversion if you like, of a convention only for perlocutionary acts (1962, 120–1). While illocutionary acts will cite and iterate conventions to enact their performative force, perlocutionary acts will derive their force from the unconventional, undecidable, and unpredictable effects (in Butler's sense of resignification). Contra Bourdieu, this is exactly where Butler locates the agency of the subject not as a sovereign subject but a speaking subject that *becomes* responsible for what it cites, repeats, and resignifies ([1997] 2021, 16). Thus, as opposed to locutionary and illocutionary acts, perlocutionary acts will rupture conventions, and their performative force will derive from this rupture. Following Derrida, Butler says: 'The force of the performative is thus not inherited from prior usage, but issues forth precisely from its break with any and all prior usage. That break, that force of rupture, is the force of the performative, beyond all question of truth or meaning' ([1997] 2021, 152). For political subjectivity, 'performativity can work in precisely such counter-hegemonic ways. That moment in which a speech act without prior authorization nevertheless assumes authorization in the course of its performance may anticipate and instate altered contexts for its future reception' (Butler [1997] 2021, 164). To conceive rupture as a complete break is not necessary. Rather, rupture is a moment where the future breaks through into the present (Deleuze [1990a] 1995, 170). It is that moment where it becomes possible to *do* something different in or by *saying* something different.

If for Austin, speech acts mean that 'in' and 'by' saying something, we are doing something, the idea that speech is not only a description (constative) but also an act (performative), ushers in a radically different way of thinking about not only speaking but also doing things in or by speaking. As Felman writes, Austin '[demystified] ... the illusion upheld by the history of philosophy according to which the only thing at stake in language is its "truth" or "falsity"' ([1980] 2003, 6). Felman showed that Austin questioned the difference between speaking and doing. Felman writes:

> If the problem of the human act thus consists in the relation between language and body, it is because the act is conceived – by performative analysis as well as by psychoanalysis – as that which problematises at the same time the separation and the opposition between the two. The act, an enigmatic and problematic production of the *speaking body*, destroys from its inception the metaphysical dichotomy between the domain of the "mental" and the domain of the "physical," breaks down the opposition between body and spirit, between matter and language.
>
> ([1980] 2003, 65, emphasis original)

Moreover, Felman considers this as 'Austinian materialism is a materialism of the residue, that is, literally, of the trivial: a materialism of the speaking body' ([1980] 2003, 109). For Austin, even constative speech acts that are statements describing a state of affairs cannot remain without effects. It is in this sense that Austin makes us think about ourselves as those beings who always know how to do things with words, even though our chances of accomplishing things we set out to do remain precarious since our words will occasionally (perhaps more so than we would like) misfire and accomplish things we did not intend.

But what about saying something in or by doing something? Or, to put it differently, what about saying something in or by doing things? This question may appear redundant since Austin is said to have questioned the difference between saying and doing. But Austin never considers speech situations where things perform words. It was Bruno Latour who raised the question of how we may accomplish words in or by doing things – hence reversing Austin's phrasing (2000). Latour's reminder that actions can accomplish words is crucial. This reversal enables us to address a question we have not yet articulated. It is the question of acting bodies. Now Austin does not explain what is an action that accomplishes an act. He implicitly recognises that action is a bodily movement that accomplishes something, but he does not explicitly recognise that to perform an act involves bodily movements. We may raise our hand, for example, in a particular way to indicate we are taking an oath – an act of promising. Here, raising a hand is an action, but the conventions governing the situation indicate that this action is performing an act of promise. An action is a bodily movement that accomplishes something. Strangely, Austin says to perform illocutionary acts does not require action. This is because the illocutionary force of an act consists in its potential. When I say, 'I promise', I indicate that in saying so I commit myself to doing something. But this act of commitment is as yet unfulfilled, and its completion is not guaranteed because I have not fulfilled it *yet*. What I have done is place myself under an obligation. By contrast, the accomplishment of a perlocutionary act requires action. Doing something means performing an action. This is strange because, as Butler says, 'when one declares that one is a homosexual, the declaration is the performative act – not the homosexuality, unless we want to claim that homosexuality is itself nothing but a kind of declaration, which would be an odd move to make' ([1997] 2021, 22). So the question of the body should make us think about the difference between speech and bodies, acts and action.

The importance of recognising that we know how to do not only things with words but also words with things was apparent in our discussion of the fractures of citizenship as an apparatus of government. If for Felman 'the scandal [of the body] consists in the fact that the act *cannot know what it is doing*' ([1980] 2003, 67, emphasis original), we need to recognize here that when bodies act, they are not only doing by speaking but also speaking by doing. This is the principal reason we need to investigate not only things done in or by speaking but also things said in or by doing things.

These issues have been repeated, cited, iterated, and resignified by Austin's recent interlocutors. What we gather from Austin, Bourdieu, Butler, Derrida, Felman, and Latour for resignifying acts for our purposes is the following. Since we act of, in, and by saying something, language calls us into being as speaking subjects of acts. To be addressed by and addressing others in language is a social act (Bourdieu). It involves our bodies not as always already given but as *responsive* agents (Butler). It involves our subjectivity (the way in which we understand our bodies and their embeddedness with others through language) not as always already given but as *responsible* agents (Butler). Being responsive means being called upon by others and to call upon others. We accomplish acts through conventions. Yet we cannot control or master our responsiveness: how we cite, iterate, and resignify conventions. We fail. This is the scandal of the body (Felman). This is the scandal of submission. Yet we make choices on what to cite, how to iterate, and where to repeat. We perform our responsibility in resignifying the conventions by which to act. This creates a space for agency. It also creates a time for rupture by which conventions are deconstructed by performative force (Derrida). This creates the space for subversion (Butler). We succeed. There are distinctions between speech acts and actions (Butler). We not only in or by saying something do things but also in or by doing things say something (Latour).

Acts of citizenship rupture both citizenship (in) law by transgressing or subverting it and citizenship (in) practice by breaking conventions. This recognises that people will perform as citizens whether they are designated as citizens or noncitizens. Acts of citizenship always occur in the gap between citizenship (in) law and citizenship (in) practice or between citizenship (in) theory and citizenship (in) practice. Acts of citizenship are irreducible to citizenship (in) practice for the latter involves habits and habitus that acts of citizenship rupture. Theorising rupture provides a necessary glimpse of a gap between how citizenship (in) law regulates subjects of rights and how citizenship (in) practice shapes and transforms citizenship (in) law. To put it differently, acts of citizenship fracture becoming citizens (in) practice and (in) theory, which gets embodied in citizenship (in) law. We shall now turn our attention to the movements through which citizenship as an apparatus of government is rendered sensible and intelligible. We shall then return to the question of rupture as a possibility of revolutionary becoming and becoming revolutionary.

Chapter 3

The senses of enacting citizenship

By exploring the sites where citizenship as an apparatus of government is assembled and emphasising acts of citizenship, we have seen the complex ways in which citizenship plays out for domination and emancipation. We want to see now how citizenship as an apparatus of government becomes sensible and intelligible. We have seen how this apparatus conceals itself by partitioning, individuating, and aggregating peoples, and atomising and isolating their experiences of citizenship. Another way of saying this is that the functioning of citizenship as an apparatus of government depends on its ability to render itself nonsensible and unintelligible. We have captured this operation with a convention of (in) for exploring how citizenship as an apparatus of government is assembled across distinct but overlapping sites. This is an operation that proceeds in all sites of citizenship, but it is especially intense in citizenship (in) law by partitioning the whole of the people into parts through laws of citizenship and individuating and aggregating them in citizenship laws. This is also an operation that never succeeds. This is the meaning of cracks or fractures in the apparatus. Citizenship as an apparatus becomes sensible and intelligible through making its lines of fracture visible, articulable, and sayable. When citizenship becomes sensible and intelligible its concealments are revealed by citizens and noncitizens with their acts of citizenship for making rights claims.

We now turn our attention to how citizenship as an apparatus of government is rendered sensible and intelligible. We will discuss five movements through which this happens: (1) when citizenship involves political and social struggles over who may and may not act as a subject of rights (i.e., to have a right to be recognized as a people before the law); (2) when these struggles include not only citizens but also noncitizens as categories of people; (3) when citizens and noncitizens generate heterogenous and transversal categories to include diverse peoples making rights claims; (4) when people act *as* citizens of, in, and by exercising, claiming, and

DOI: 10.4324/9781003395997-4

performing rights and obligations, and; (5) when people act *as* citizens by making rights claims creatively transforming the meanings of its apparatus and opening cracks in its functions.

Citizenship provokes social struggles

The first movement through which citizenship is rendered sensible is that of the struggles over who may or may not act as citizens: people demand their right to make rights claims. Citizenship signifies both a struggle (making rights claims) and what that struggle performatively brings into being (the right to claim rights). If we recall how, 500 or so years ago first in Euro-America and then 250 years ago across the world, the state (especially the nation-state) became the dominant polity, we must recognise how citizenship as an apparatus of government aims to constitute a people as the people as a whole and partitions peoples. The attributes of a social group, however defined (e.g., propertied, adult, male, 'rational', white, Christian, heterosexual, and able-bodied), become the dominant attributes of the citizen as such or the people as a whole. These attributes were based on the subjection or subjectivation of various subaltern parts as subjects with limited (or without) rights (e.g., the poor, the youth, the idle, the dangerous, workers, women, irrational, racialised, non-Christian, Muslim, indigenous, Jewish, queers, lesbians, gays, bisexuals, transgender, questioning, intersex, disabled, animals, plants, mountains, and rivers). These were regarded as parts incapable of fulfilling the obligations of citizenship and hence acting as citizens. As we discussed, citizenship as an apparatus of government makes these people up by partitioning, individuating, and aggregating them into various positions.

Although there were always precedents, it was in the last 75 years that the emancipation struggles for civil, political, social, and sexual rights started to significantly challenge this. These struggles began unravelling the dominant attributes of citizenship, and the unravelling is still under way albeit against resistance. For now, some claims to citizenship remain as precarious as ever. Youth, children, disabled, Muslims, the poor, indigenous, racialised, women, queers, migrants – in any combination of these – are making (or rejecting) rights claims, so that they might cross lines from precarious to at least more liveable positions. We are also witnessing the deprivation of rights such as revocation of citizenship and regression of rights that were successfully claimed (e.g., reproductive rights for women).

We have also seen how citizenship as an apparatus of government makes itself unsensible and unintelligible. We now want to focus on how it also provokes struggles to render it sensible and intelligible. To do this we need to have our first discussion about the revolts, protests, and uprisings that make citizenship sensible and intelligible. Arendt ([1963] 1990) makes a provocative suggestion that although there have been revolts, protests, uprisings, and occupations by the subaltern to resist domination these have never been – until 1789 – about bringing something new into being, ushering in a new order of government. This is because Arendt thinks that historically the poor and slaves were never constituted as subjects of emancipation until about 200 years ago, as the differences between the rich and poor were naturalised. Words such as 'rebellion' and 'revolt' never indicated emancipation as revolutions have been understood since 1789 (Arendt [1963] 1990, 40). Arendt was certain that liberation in the revolutionary sense meant that the oppressed and the repressed peoples would rise and become sovereign ([1963] 1990, 40). For Arendt this would be equivalent to all peoples of Rome or Athens including not only all citizens but also noncitizens such as the slaves and aliens rising and demanding an equality of rights. And Arendt thought that this never happened (40).

Arendt separates those who are part of the whole already (populus, demos) and those who are outside (slaves, aliens). Arendt recognises that the polities after the decline of Greek and Roman polities also experienced rebellion and revolts, defiance, and disobedience but 'the aim of such rebellions was not a challenge of authority or the established order of things as such' (40); rather it was always an uprising against an authority (e.g., king, tyrant) but not against a regime as such.

For Arendt, it was only when people began doubting that poverty is inherent or natural that the struggles of the poor and slaves demanded emancipation ([1963] 1990, 22–3). For Arendt,

> The modern concept of revolution, inextricably bound up with the notion that the course of history suddenly begins anew, that an entirely new story, a story never known or told before, is about to unfold, was unknown prior to the two great revolutions at the end of the eighteenth century.
>
> ([1963] 1990, 28)

There are two aspects of Arendt's argument on revolution that concern us from the perspective of developing a concept of citizenship as an apparatus of government and how it provokes social and political struggles. The first is the view that revolution is a spectacular displacement and overturning of power that traverses the people as a whole. We will return to this view in our discussion of citizenship as a revolutionary subjectivity. The second aspect of Arendt's argument about revolution concerns how partitioning, individuating, and aggregating a people is its condition of possibility. This second aspect is vague but, in our view, it becomes apparent if we understand why Arendt was so passionately critical about human rights. Arendt's argument that the French Revolution had already (at least partially) replaced a concrete conception of the citizen subject with an abstract conception of the human subject and that The Universal Declaration of Human Rights (1948) ostensibly universalising this abstract human subject can be distilled into this: that this abstract human subject rendered impossible the partitioning, individuating, and aggregating peoples with discernible principles.

For Arendt the invention of the category 'displaced persons' to replace 'statelessness' was a turning point in the formation of the abstract human subject. For her the category 'stateless' at least acknowledges that people were partitioned outside a polity and transnational or international agreements were required to protect them. The category 'displaced persons was invented during the war for the express purpose of liquidating statelessness once and for all by ignoring its existence' (Arendt 1951, 279). This enabled polities to partition peoples outside politics and without protection. As a result, we have now 'reached the point where even free democracies as, for instance, the United States, were seriously considering depriving native Americans who are communists of their citizenship. The sinister aspect of these measures is that they are being considered in all innocence' (Arendt 1951, 280).

Arendt emphatically recalls that the Nazis had insisted that all Jews of non-German nationality were deprived of their citizenship either before, or on the day of deportation (1951, 280). She adds that 'for German Jews such a decree was not needed, because in the Third Reich there existed a law according to which all Jews who had left the territory – including, of course, those deported to a Polish camp – automatically lost their citizenship) in order to realize the true implications of statelessness' (280).

For Arendt this episode signals the end of '[the] long and sacred history of asylum [dating] back to the very beginnings of regulated political life' (1951, 280). She argues that 'since ancient times' asylum has protected peoples becoming outlaws through circumstances beyond their control (280).

Yet, it was distressing that 'the right to asylum could …not be found in written law, in no constitution or international agreement, and the Covenant of the League of Nations never even so much as mentioned it' (Arendt 1951, 280).

This development led to the question of protecting the rights of citizens being transformed into a question of the police. For Arendt,

> The nation-state, incapable of providing a law for those who had lost the protection of a national government, transferred the whole matter to the police. This was the first time the police in Western Europe had received authority to act on its own, to rule directly over people; in one sphere of public life it was no longer an instrument to carry out and enforce the law but had become a ruling authority independent of government and ministries. Its strength and its emancipation from law and government grew in direct proportion to the influx of refugees.
>
> (1951, 287)

To put it differently, citizenship as an apparatus of government enacted a *persona ficta* of the people as the sovereign, partitioned some people as outlaws, individuated them as refugees, and aggregated them as displaced. The consequence of this was that the '[citizen] had hardly appeared as a completely emancipated, completely isolated being who carried his dignity within himself without reference to some larger encompassing order, when he disappeared again into a member of a people' (Arendt 1951, 291).

If the problem of the declaration of human rights for Arendt was the replacement of a concrete citizen subject with an abstract human subject, the consequences of this became obvious when a growing number of people and peoples suddenly appeared without rights in Europe (1951, 291). Yet, 'the Rights of Man, supposedly inalienable, proved to be unenforceable – even in countries whose constitutions were based upon them – whenever people appeared who were no longer citizens of any sovereign state' (Arendt 1951, 293).

It was impossible to distinguish with any precision between abstract rights of the human subject from the concrete rights of the citizen subject: 'although everyone seems to agree that the plight of these people consists precisely in their loss of [human rights], no one seems to know which rights they lost when they lost these human rights' (Arendt 1951, 293).

It was only when millions of people who had lost and could not regain their rights that 'we became aware of the existence of a right to have rights (and that means to live in a framework where one is judged by one's actions and opinions) and a right to belong to some kind of organized community' (1951, 296–7).

This concept of citizenship by Arendt as 'the right to have rights' expresses the right to belong to a polity not as a member of an abstract category but as a citizen. If for Arendt 'the world found nothing sacred in the abstract nakedness of being human' (Arendt 1951, 298), it was because the world forgot that citizenship meant being part of a polity. It was obvious to Arendt that if a human being loses their political status, they should, according to the implications of the inborn and inalienable human rights come under exactly the situation for which the declarations of such general rights provided. Actually, the opposite is the case: 'It seems that a man who is nothing but a man has lost the very qualities which make it possible for other people to treat him as a fellow-man' (Arendt 1951, 300). From our perspective of citizenship as an apparatus of government, what Arendt attempts here is to suture the fracture between the people as a whole and peoples as its parts. She imagines that citizenship was an undifferentiated, indivisible, and univocal position. Yet, as we argue here, citizenship was invented as an apparatus of government to create the people as a whole, to partition people into its parts, and hierarchically distribute rights and obligations. Is it possible to suture this fracture? So what appears paradoxical to Arendt appears as a political assemblage to us. Citizenship as an apparatus partitions, individuates, and aggregates peoples, and emancipation from its capture means calling into question the assemblage of this apparatus.

Jacques Rancière approaches Arendt's (1951, 290–302) argument about human rights from a perspective of politics constituted through struggles (of those who have no part yet who make themselves count). Rancière thinks Arendt finds human rights perplexing because she understands human rights only in legal and not performative mode. Rancière does not think that there is an antinomy between human rights and citizenship rights. Arendt, Rancière says, assumes that 'either [human rights are] the rights of those who have no rights or the rights of those who [already] have rights [who are citizens]' (2004, 302). Instead, Rancière proposes that 'the rights of [humans] are the rights of those who have not the rights that they have and have the rights that they have not' (2004, 302). This formulation has two parts. The first concerns those rights that are enacted by subjects who are not included in what counts as subjects of these rights. The second concerns those rights enacted by subjects who are counted in what counts, but who do not have the rights that they are supposed to have. When subjects are acting *as* citizen subjects, it is not even imagined or imaginable – given how a polity is instituted – that they have a right to do so. When subjects perform themselves as citizen subjects their acts become political. Acts *of* citizenship are about bringing these forces into being. When citizen subjects claim 'I, we, or they have a right to', they are claiming both rights they don't have and rights they do have. Rancière illustrates this with women's rights. First, women demonstrate that they are denied the rights that they have by referring to the declaration of rights. This is to say, if indeed rights are universal (as affirmed by declarations), then women (should) have a right to count themselves in those rights. Second, women can also enact rights that are already in the declaration naming them. So Rancière says that '[women] could act as subjects of the rights of [humans] in the precise sense that ... they acted as subjects that did not have the rights that they had and had the rights that they had not' (2004, 304). Thus, 'political subjects are not definite collectivities. They are surplus names, names that set out a question or a dispute about who is included in their count' (Rancière 2004, 303).

From our perspective of developing a concept of citizenship as an apparatus of government, we do not see fractures of citizenship as paradoxes and perplexities but as already assembled into the apparatus itself. What appear as paradoxes are fractures that make citizenship as an apparatus sensible and intelligible. When people enact rights that they do not have and rights that they should have, they make themselves into citizen subjects who cannot be known in advance. Their acts are struggles over how citizenship as an apparatus partitions, individuates, and aggregates them. To put it slightly differently, the force of rights derives from citizenship (in) law between their inscription (acts *on* citizenship) and enactment (acts *of* citizenship). For Rancière, 'these rights are theirs when they can do something with them to construct a dissensus against the denial of rights they suffer' (2004, 305–6). And, perhaps more importantly, 'there are always people among them who do it' (2004, 306). The key question, 'Who is the subject of rights?' goes amiss. We mentioned earlier that the bills, conventions, charters, and declarations claiming rights – with all the events associated with them in Table 0.3 – are about repeatedly enacting the imaginary of rights as a contested field of social and political struggles whose causes and effects make the citizen subject. Yet, the citizen subject disappears from the charters claiming rights and instead is replaced by the human rights of 'individuals'. This radically shifts the performative force of these declarations to affirm and assert the citizen as both the subject of these rights, not merely as a subject of nationality (nation-state), or a subject of humanity (human rights), or a bearer (or holder) of rights but as a historical subject that we inherit and who has a right to claim rights.

The gap between enactment (acts of citizenship) and inscription (acts on citizenship) of rights always remains open. Those whose attempt to inscribe rights in law work with the assumption that their enactment will follow their inscription. Those whose acts enact rights work with the conviction that their inscription will follow their enactment. Yet, their inscription is a prelude to their enactment while their enactment inspires their inscription.

Citizenship produces both citizens and noncitizens

The second movement through which citizenship becomes sensible is when its apparatus generates both citizens and noncitizens. The parts of the whole often occupy different and overlapping or intersecting positions ranging from citizens (insiders) to noncitizens (strangers, outsiders, and aliens). We have already suggested that citizens are those subjects whose entitlements and privileges are instituted as civil, political, social, and sexual rights. Often, some people, while they may be accepted into citizenship in the future, are still considered strangers in the sense that they have not yet fulfilled requirements to act as citizens. Consider, for example, women (200 years ago in Britain), African Americans (100 years ago in America), and indigenous peoples (in settler colonial polities such as Canada and Australia) as peoples that were deemed strangers because dominant people constituted them as lacking capacities. Yet both women and later African Americans were also integrated as essential parts of the polity that fulfilled functions for it (reproduction for women as mothers, labour for 'blacks' as slaves first and then as workers). By contrast, those peoples who are deemed outsiders to citizenship may find themselves as migrants and refugees struggling for the right to be present or exist in a polity at all. To understand how citizenship as an apparatus of government interpellates and constitutes not only citizens (insiders) but also a range of noncitizens (strangers, outsiders, and aliens), we return to Arendt who suggests that slaves or aliens only revolted against wrongs and that only since 1789 have the poor and the dispossessed been able to revolt for a revolution. This suggestion should now appear questionable. Citizenship as an apparatus of government interpellates both citizens and noncitizens and a range of hierarchies instituted to distribute their rights. It is certainly possible to consider revolutionary claims by noncitizens.

Citizenship as an apparatus of government often draws the line between strangers and outsiders along disposability and deportability: strangers (such as slaves in the American South) are sometimes accepted as indispensable, whereas outsiders may become indispensable too but are seen as remaining outside disciplinary reform and thus sequestered. Jews were ascribed to this category in most of European history and indigenous peoples in Euro-American history. This line makes citizenship as an apparatus of government a dynamic play of domination and emancipation rather than a static apparatus. If those treated as aliens in a polity typically face total rejection but question why they are seen as continuing to pose a threat when they remain in the territory, they articulate themselves as noncitizen claimants. Even categories such as enemy combatants or terrorists, examples of parts regarded as irredeemable and whose citizenship is often subject to revocation or denaturalisation, can constitute themselves as claimants.

Citizenship as an apparatus of government creates the categories of citizens, strangers, outsiders, and aliens and renders them as objects of social struggles. An immense variety of peoples are partitioned, individuated, and aggregated into these categories. The boundaries between citizens, strangers, outsiders, and aliens always change precisely because they are objects of struggles. As we have already mentioned, people identify with or are ascribed to various social groups and constantly traverse the boundaries separating citizens and noncitizens (strangers, outsiders, and aliens). Moving across these positions or breaking down the boundaries between them involves struggles over rights.

Governing ourselves as subjects of and to power therefore means performing rights that we may have (e.g., the right to vote) and claiming rights that we may not have (e.g., the right to same-sex marriage). It also means making claims for or against rights that other 'subjects' do not have (e.g., animal or robot rights).

We have so far discussed citizenship as though each polity develops its conventions of citizenship. Yet, many social groups, even those defined as nations, exist across not only borders but also orders. This gives rise to numerous fractures of citizenship. The sovereign state became the dominant polity in modernity through a history involving colonialism, imperialism, and nationalism. Euro-American empires have left indelible marks on polities they colonised and have imposed various citizenship arrangements on them. These arrangements erased or displaced already existing political and social relations between and amongst various social groups and replaced them with forms of imperial and colonial citizenship. These indelible marks of colonialism have not only inscribed names – such as America, Africa, Asia, and the Middle East – but also citizenship arrangements whose legacies remain today. Thus, the complex and enduring history of citizenship is not merely world history but also an earth history.

The citizen and noncitizen arrangements that obtained in each polity were disseminated across the metropole and the colony, creating spatio-temporal arrangements of citizens and their others (strangers, outsiders, aliens). The colonised subjects were seen to have never understood or developed the capabilities of citizenship and its ostensible unifying powers. If colonial subjects were deemed to have understood citizenship, it was because it was 'borrowed' in postcolonial sovereign states. This makes studying citizenship in colonial and postcolonial states a vexed activity. Is the description 'what citizens and noncitizens perform in making rights claims' adequate to study citizenship in colonial and postcolonial states?

Citizenship involves making rights claims

The third movement through which citizenship becomes sensible is when it involves making rights claims. We have already seen that making rights claims concerns both the content of rights and what people are doing when they perform citizenship. Making rights claims is a concept that arises from social movement studies, which, for 75 years or so, focused on the injustices people suffer and how they fight against the denial of rights to them and others (Berger and Nehring 2017). Since then, we have come to recognise that citizenship signifies both a struggle (making rights claims) and what that struggle performatively brings into being (the right to claim rights). This distinction is politically and theoretically significant.

The distinction between claiming to be a subject of rights and making rights claims is essential for understanding acts of citizenship. The distinction enables us to study how people stage creative and transformative resistances and articulate claims against domination and the injustices it precipitates and whether this leads to emancipation. The focus is not only on the performativity of rights and obligations as they exist but also on claiming rights and obligations yet to come. As Karen Zivi (2012, 8) writes, 'to approach rights and rights claiming from the perspective of performativity means, then, asking questions not simply about what a right is but also about what it is we do when we make rights claims'. This distinction emphasises that, when performing the right to claim rights, there is an implicit claim to equality between citizens and noncitizens. This means that citizens and noncitizens are both performing a transversal right to claim rights but in different and diverse ways.

This distinction raises the question of how subjects become citizen subjects. Does it always have the structure of a protest, resistance, or revolt? Can an act of submission also function as a creative act despite its negative connotation? We have already mentioned that the exercise of power involves modes of performativity. When we are studying the ways in which citizenship as an apparatus is rendered sensible and intelligible, we would need a situated approach to see how modes of exercising power, obedience, submission, and subversion, can have diverse effects for domination or emancipation. We will now need to return to Austin in search of the performativity of making claims. We will see that it is surprisingly absent despite his detailed examination of modes of performativity in speech acts.

To begin with, Austin or his interlocutors often do not speak about citizen subjects making rights claims. Butler comes closest since she is interested in articulating a 'politics of the performative', but her primary concern is not the citizen subject as such who claims 'I, we, they have a right to'. We will return to the argument that making rights claims involves in or by saying and doing 'I, we, they have a right to'. We can now add that citizen subjects who make such claims should not be conflated with the rights-bearing subjects who already exist and whose claim is to already existing rights. On the contrary, citizen subjects performatively come into being in or by the act of saying something – whether through words, images, or other things – and, in doing so, open possibilities.

To understand citizen subjects who make rights claims by saying and doing 'I, we, they have a right to', we are moving from the first person to the second and the third, from the individual to the collective. We need to consider two additional forces that make acts possible. The two forces are the force of the law and the force of the imaginary. Arguably, numerous examples that Austin provides address the force of law. Austin calls two classes of speech acts judgements and decisions, and regarding judgements, most of his examples are court verdicts. Yet we still think that the performative force of a convention's legality is different enough that the force of law should be considered as a separate force. Breaking a convention will have significantly different effects, depending upon whether that convention is constituted as legal or illegal.

The imaginary is undeniably a significant force in making an act possible, which Austin does not consider. Cornelius Castoriadis asks a simple and yet quite a challenging question: what holds together any given thing called a polity? What gives a polity its apparent cohesion, unity, and organisation? ([1975] 1987, 3–18). Castoriadis says that we ought to understand the social institution of imaginary as that which holds a polity together. The institution does not mean organisations but conventions by which individuals and groups conduct themselves. The social institution of imaginary requires norms, values, language, tools, procedures, and methods of dealing with relations and differentiations – in short, apparatuses. Any apparatus requires coercion and sanctions but also support, adherence, legitimacy, belief, and consensus. It cultivates individuals and groups who know how to negotiate these sanctions and adherences. The institution of polity through which individuals and groups conduct themselves through conventions would be impossible without what Castoriadis calls social imaginary. These include spirits, gods, God, polis, citizen, nation, state, party, commodity, money, capital, interest, taboo, virtue, sin, and so forth. These are imaginaries not because they fail to correspond to concrete and specific experiences or things but because they require acts of imagination. They are social because they are instituted and maintained by collectivities. They are political because they cultivate modes of conduct. Being both social and political, these institute polity as coherent and unified yet always incoherent and fragmented. How each polity deals with this tension constitutes its politics. Castoriadis thinks that this tension is especially acute in democracy as it cultivates a citizen who remains at home with this tension. The citizen is autonomous not because it is separate or independent from polity, but as its product, it retains the capability to question its own institution. Castoriadis says that this new type of being (the citizen subject) is capable of calling into question the very laws of its existence and has created the possibility of both deliberation and political action. The imaginary institution of society for Castoriadis is much more complex than we portray it here, but what we want to recognise is that not only does the social institution of an imaginary require making and cracking apparatuses, but these apparatuses can be sustained only through the force of the imaginary: myths, stories, and values that inhabit people and their sense of the world and the earth.

How the citizen subject comes into being through enacting themselves reveals that the citizen subject is both a result and an effect of making claims about rights that may or may not yet exist. By making rights claims in or by saying and doing 'I, we, they have a right to', people enact themselves as citizen subjects. To put it differently, it is by making rights claims, by the forces through which people enact those claims that they bring themselves into being as citizen subjects.

We need to return to Austin briefly and then show how his classification of speech acts requires expansion to understand citizen subjects making rights claims in or by saying and doing something. Of interest here are what Austin considers as five classes of acts with performative force: judgements, decisions, commitments, acknowledgements, and clarifications. (1) There are judgements, such as acquitting, convicting, measuring, characterising, ranking, calculating, and placing. These are typified by giving a verdict. As we mentioned earlier, we separate judgements in citizenship (in) law, citizenship (on) practice, citizenship (in) theory and citizenship (in) acts. (2) There are decisions, such as appointing, excommunicating, sentencing, nominating, resigning, bequeathing, pleading, and pardoning. These are typified by exercising power, influence, and authority. (3) There are commitments, such as guaranteeing, pledging, consenting, espousing, embracing, and proposing. Promising or undertaking to commit to doing something typifies these. These also include declarations or announcements of intention. (4) There are acknowledgements, such as apologising, congratulating, commending, cursing, and challenging. They are typified by action that involves socially oriented and evaluated expression. (5) There are clarifications, such as conceding, illustrating, assuming, postulating, or replying. They are typified by the declarations 'I argue', 'I postulate' (Austin 1962, 153–62).

This classification of acts is clearly useful for developing our view on acts of citizen subjects and how they crack citizenship as an apparatus of government. Yet, Austin (and his interlocutors) do not pay enough, if any, attention to the subject who thus speaks 'I, we, or they have a right to' (see Austin 1962, 156). What kinds of acts are those that make rights claims? They are not judgements, decisions, commitments, acknowledgements, or clarifications. They are claims. When Karen Zivi argues for a performative approach to understanding rights, she suggests that 'it means asking questions about what we are doing together when we say we have rights, about the realities we create and the relationships we engender through the making of rights claims, and about the effects that our utterances may have, intended or otherwise, on both ourselves and others' (Zivi 2012, 19). This, in turn, for Zivi, requires 'appreciating the extent to which our claims both reference and reiterate social conventions and norms, and yet have forces and effects that exceed them' (Zivi 2012, 19) Thus, she argues that we should

> treat claims such as 'I have a right to privacy' or 'We have a right to health care' as performative utterances, asking not just whether the particular claim corresponds to law or morality as if it were simply a constative utterance but also what it is a speaker does in or by making a particular claim. We need to analyze making rights claims, in other words, as an illocutionary and a perlocutionary activity.
> (Zivi 2012, 15)

Yet, ironically, as we mentioned above, as a class of speech acts, claiming is not on Austin's list.

We have already suggested, as a first move, expanding the forces that make speech acts possible. Having proposed that, we now name the class of acts that involves 'making rights claims' as 'claims'. In other words, we are proposing to add a new class of acts to Austin's: claims. It is this new class of acts that interpellate citizen subjects and enable them to render citizenship as an apparatus of government sensible and intelligible. People making rights claims in or by saying 'I, we, they have a right to' enact themselves as citizen subjects. It is necessary to reflect further on how in or by saying and doing 'I, we, or they have a right to' a citizen subject is produced.

The citizen subject, we have argued, can be both a submissive and subversive speaking subject. How does 'I, we, or they have a right to' *function* as a claim? First, it places the citizen subject under conventions that constitute callings on them. Making rights claims in or by saying 'I, we, or they have a right to', the citizen subject recognises – explicitly or tacitly, consciously or unconsciously – that they act under certain conventions. Saying 'I have a right to' is possible only within an apparatus from which it derives its force. This is an act of submission, which is also a creative act despite its negative image. We discussed earlier how power can be exercised through separate but related modes of obedience, submission, and subversion.

Yet, and second, the utterance 'I, we, or they have a right to' also provokes closings or openings. What we mean by this is that as a claim, the utterance 'have a right to' places demands on the other to act in a particular way. This can activate the force of the law, for example, when citizen subjects claim that a right is being violated. Or it can mobilise a performative force in or by breaking a convention. Or it can invoke an imaginary force by appealing to a convention that is out of place or time. This is the sense in which the rights of a subject are obligations on others and the rights of others function as obligations on us. By virtue of the legal, performative, or imaginary forces, 'I, we, or they have a right to' can provoke openings and closings as possibilities. The conversion between submission and subversion can be instantaneous. In or by saying and doing something and making rights claims as a speaking citizen subject may have aimed at subversion of a convention, yet it may well have functioned, as a misfire would, as an act of submission to that convention. Or an act of obedience, for that matter. How an act functions in making rights claims through interpellations, closings, and openings and how a citizen subject is produced through these are matters of investigation.

By adding claims as a class of acts to Austin's judgements, decisions, commitments, acknowledgements, and clarifications, we have identified making rights claims with 'I, we, they have a right to' as acts of citizenships that bring citizen subjects into being. This is another way of seeing how citizenship as an apparatus of government is open to both domination and emancipation and making rights claims renders this apparatus sensible and intelligible.

Jacques Derrida's remarkably short piece on the Declaration of Independence illustrates the force of claims as a class of acts (1986). It was Derrida who thought that such declarations as speech acts could be considered in their performative force for the effects that they create (1986, 7). He thought that a declaration such as the Declaration of Independence cannot be read as a constative speech act describing the state of affairs of which it speaks but should be read as a performative act, which 'performs, it accomplishes, it does what it says it does; that at least would be its intentional structure' (Derrida 1986, 8). The question that concerns Derrida is 'Who is the actual signer of such acts?' (1986, 8). If indeed a declaration constitutes a claim 'I, we, they have a right to', the question becomes: by what right do these signatories constitute themselves as political subjects? When a declaration such as this is claimed, one cannot know whether its performative force is able to produce the effect that it promises, that of instituting a political subject of rights. Even if it is done in the name of the people, a declaration has no way of guaranteeing that in fact its people exist or will exist as a fact. Rather, and this is Derrida's intervention, the act brings the people, its political subject, into being through the act. The people a declaration names does not exist. Derrida writes, '[People] [does] not exist as an entity, it does not exist, before this declaration, not as such. If it gives birth to itself, as free and independent subject, as possible signer, this can hold only in the act of the signature. The signature invents the signer' (1986, 10). That the signature invents the signer can be easily misinterpreted to mean that before the signature, the signer does not exist; but it means that 'there was no signer, by right, before the text of the Declaration which itself remains the producer and guarantor of its own signature' (Derrida 1986, 10). On the contrary, the signature gives itself a name, a name by which a people, a citizen subject, is named. The force of a declaration, its performative 'force makes right, founds right or the law, gives right, brings the law to the light of day, gives both birth and day to the law' (Derrida 1986, 10–11). By bringing into play a chain of events, delegation, representation, naming, signature, and citations, a declaration enacts a signature that restores, by right, their subjectivity to citizen subjects.

Derrida provides two important lessons about acts of citizenship. First, it is undecidable whether an act is indeed capable of producing a subject that it names. For that reason, without guarantees, it must be done regardless of its actual effects, for the effects of citation and iteration are as much about bringing the citizen subject thus named into being as about trying to remind ourselves that 'I, we, they have a right to' must be performed. Second, without naming the citizen subject, without citing and iterating yet again that 'I, we, they have a right to', its eventual effect will not be accomplished, that is, bringing the force of law into being. With Rancière, we can say that staging this dissensus brings together the two necessary aspects of a declaration as a performative act and bridges the gap between inscription and enactment. So, although we said that bills, charters, declarations, and manifestos enact an imaginary force by which citizen subjects are named and claims made, we must now recognise that indeed without the imaginary force of these bills, charters, declarations, and manifestos, there can be no performative or legal effects that bring its citizen subjects into being.

Our argument is that bills, charters, declarations, and manifestos as major acts of citizenship would indeed have stronger imaginary force if they also derived their performative force from minor acts of citizenship: how people take up positions as citizens, how they respond to callings to participate, how they create openings for constituting themselves differently, how they struggle for and against closings, and how they make rights claims in or by performing digital acts.

These acts of citizenship would have more performative if not legal force if they arose from not only major acts but also minor acts for understanding how the citizen subject is being articulated differently and how the citizen subject is essential for bringing the force of law into being. The most significant space for thinking about the politics of citizenship as an apparatus of government and the citizen subject it produces is the gap between the inscription of rights and their enactment. Those who imagine the inscription of rights will bring about their realisation often assume that the fact of this inscription is also their guarantee. This may not be stated explicitly, but the discourse on inscribing rights often assumes that the force of such laws will guarantee that individuals, states, companies, and other bodies will perform them. This assumption fails to recognise that how people experience being citizens and how they perform rights by bringing them into being through enacting themselves are the grounds on which rights will be guaranteed. How people experience performing rights is the key to understanding how they inhabit that space of rights and develop a political subjectivity necessary to making rights claims 'I, we, they have a right to'. Without such understanding and without developing concepts and methods appropriate to such an understanding, most efforts to inscribe rights, we are afraid, would remain inadequate, for these would be rights without political subjects. Conversely, the same can be said for those who assume that the enactment of rights, of imaginatively and performatively bringing rights into being, would guarantee their inscription. Without understanding the legality of claims and their scope or substance, such enactments would remain inadequate, too. Without the force of law, this would amount to subjects without political rights. It is that space between inscription and enactment that creates tensions when citizen subjects are emerging as political subjects. Those whose politics side with either inscription or enactment are somehow missing the significance of their relation. Citizenship as an apparatus of government becomes sensible and intelligible when people make rights claims and reveal this tension between inscription and enactment. As we shall see, this is also the condition of the possibility of citizenship as a revolutionary subjectivity.

Citizenship generates both stability and instability

The fourth movement through which citizenship as an apparatus of government is rendered sensible and intelligible is when making rights claims, when people effectively demand that 'I, we, or they have a right to...', they will enact themselves as claimants whether they have that right in law or not. At the centre of enacting citizenship is the articulation of making rights claims, becoming political subjects by rendering citizenship as an apparatus of government sensible. When people make rights claims they both reference and cite rights, and yet the performative force of their claims often exceeds or breaks them. Yet, when there are clearly enabling conventions, making rights claims may still exceed those conventions.

There is a line between the right to claim rights as a universal right and making particular claims for rights. When people perform citizenship, these two poles play out and open a fracture where a social group is excluded and yet makes rights claims to political subjectivity. This is an important reason the object of analysis in studying performative citizenship is acts and how they disrupt, rupture, or break conventions. This creates instability. As citizenship as an apparatus of government makes itself nonsensible, citizens and noncitizens making rights claims makes it sensible and intelligible. This always produces instability where the apparatus must make itself sensible and intelligible in order to stabilise the situation and diffuse the tensions that arise from the instability. Thus, making citizenship as an apparatus of government sensible and intelligible renders the apparatus vulnerable, exposed, and susceptible to provocation and even transformation.

Citizenship calls (for) transversality

The fifth way in which citizenship as an apparatus of government is rendered sensible is when, through struggling for their rights, the rights of others, and the rights to come, people constitute themselves as citizens in solidarity with citizens, noncitizens, and nonhumans. This means people cross social, political, and geographic boundaries and create transversal (shared or common) struggles for equality, justice, liberty, emancipation, and solidarity. What makes citizenship performative in this sense is not only that it involves iterating or exceeding conventions about what people may and may not do but also that people often traverse polities. By so doing citizens and noncitizens, with or without rights, perform acts, traverse borders and orders, transform themselves and others, the rights by which they make claims, and the rights to which they make claims.

We have frequently mentioned that citizenship as an apparatus of government conceals its operations by partitioning, individuating, and aggregating. While peoples are interpellated into the people as whole to imagine themselves as a unified body, citizenship apparatus partitions and fragments peoples into various categories, individuates them through diverse legal fields, and aggregates them into various groups with differentiated rights. This renders citizenship as an apparatus of government unsensible and unintelligible because, while its imaginary constitutes a body politic as a whole, its constituent parts are atomised, isolated, and fragmented. Just what makes the people as a whole remains mystical or an empty signifier.

Making citizenship apparatus sensible and intelligible calls (for) transversality in two ways. First, as peoples make rights claims through atomised, isolated, or fragmented struggles, their acts of citizenship increasingly expose the fact that these specific struggles are related to other struggles. Their acts enjoin others to make claims on laws of citizenship. To put it differently, acts of citizenship transform citizenship acts. Second, their claims also expose transversal operations of power and begin to transform polities that contain them. We observe these two processes, especially how class, race and gender are unconcealed by what we shall later call planetary movements. Four transversal movements and their planetary transmissions can illustrate this: Black Lives Matter, #MeToo, No One is Illegal, and Idle No More. These movements are known, but our aim here is to mention how they traverse each other to institute a planetary imaginary of politics and citizenship and how they transform apparatuses that govern them by cracking the lines (i.e., race, gender, class) that cross them.

A revolt articulates a specific claim against the injustice of the alleged murder of a black person by police. It gradually accumulates into a systemic claim, symbolised by Black Lives Matter, which aims to show that there is a historic and systemic pattern of police brutality against black peoples. The articulation of this systemic claim does not disavow the specific claim of injustice, but it traverses through the political body as a whole. Quite rapidly, the slogan begins to interpellate similar, and more significantly, dissimilar claims against injustice traversing from race to class to gender, such as #MeToo.

A *specific* claim against harassment of women in the workplace accumulates into a *systemic* claim, #MeToo, that traverses the body of citizens. It reverberates and resonates as a movement by transmitting and disseminating both its specific and systemic claims across polities. What both movements performatively accomplish is to connect experiences from specific, atomised, and individuated situations into systemic patterns, events, and occurrences. This renders citizenship as an apparatus of government sensible and intelligible, as these claims articulate experiences of the people as a whole and not only as its parts. These movements rupture the cycle of partition, individuation, and aggregation and constitute themselves as a planetary body as a whole.

A transnational movement, 'No One is Illegal', against deportations of migrants and refugees articulates at least three principles of transversality that render citizenship as an apparatus of government sensible and intelligible. Its first principle is a transversal solidarity between citizens and noncitizens. Citizens not only claim that 'I, we, have a right to' but also 'they have a right to'. This moves the position of noncitizens from abjects (with no rights) to subjects (with noncitizen rights), and eventually to citizens (as claimants). The second principle shows the arbitrariness of criteria that breach international conventions such as non-refoulement. The third principle is embodied in the phrase 'no one'. This act imaginatively but effectively eliminates borders and orders of citizenship as an apparatus, and it imagines transversal and planetary political spaces. This new political space has no borders since everyone is declared legal in their movements.

An uprising, 'Idle No More', claiming the rights of indigenous peoples against being partitioned as indigenous, individuated as victims, and aggregated as nationals reveals how citizenship as an apparatus of government functions (Gilio-Whitaker 2015). Idle No More erupts in November 2012 as a response to a Canadian federal government bill that severely erodes indigenous sovereignty (Couture 2014). It grows not only by using the internet for organising as a resistance movement but also through hundreds of rallies, teach-ins, and protests resisting neocolonialism. It dances its way into the collective political imaginary by making rights claims and rupturing categories of noncitizenship and citizenship. What Idle No More inscribes is that the ways in which indigenous peoples have been subjected to internal colonisation can be seen as an effect of citizenship as an apparatus of government. The point here is not that there were indigenous peoples and that their rights were fought for within the constitutions of colonial and then federal governments. Rather, indigenous rights and their citizenship practices were subjected to strategies and technologies of government to extinguish, assimilate, and incorporate the rights of indigenous peoples to articulate how they want to govern themselves. The claims articulated by Idle No More are not about inclusion or recognition within Canadian citizenship but about demonstrating how Canadian citizenship as an apparatus of government constitutes indigenous peoples as its strangers and outsiders. This movement traverses movements for rights of indigenous peoples across the planet.

Chapter 4

Citizenship, a revolutionary subjectivity?

For some readers whether citizenship is a revolutionary subjectivity may be a surprising question. From everything we have argued so far about citizenship as an apparatus of government, it may appear that citizenship is a subjectivity that produces and activates governable subjects – more subject to power than subject of power and more subservient and obedient than subversive and dissenting. As citizen subjects render citizenship as an apparatus of government sensible and intelligible, it may now appear that it primarily functions for domination rather than emancipation. The recent historical development of this apparatus may have inclined toward domination rather than emancipation by creating sedimented laws, practices, and imaginaries that are far too oppressive and repressive for all those who are captured by its partitioning, individuating, and aggregating force. Yet, this apparatus has also produced an unintended consequence: the citizen as a revolutionary subject.

We have seen how citizenship as an apparatus of government embodies various fractures between nomadic and sedentary, techne and episteme, eastern and western, ancient and modern, and human and nonhuman. We traced these fractures as lines that traverse them: movement, technology, coloniality, sovereignty, and planetarity. These fractures remain wide in citizenship as an apparatus of government. As this apparatus partitions, individuates, and aggregates peoples into the people as a whole, it remains impossible to suture its fractures as they are necessary to its functioning. We have concluded that if citizenship governs the relationship between a polity, its peoples, and its species, by partitioning them into citizens (strangers), noncitizens (foreigners, aliens), and nonhuman (abjects) with or without rights and obligations, individuating them with attributes and characteristics, and aggregates them by classifications, it also opens possibilities for objection, resistance, protest, or struggle.

DOI: 10.4324/9781003395997-5

To put it differently, if citizenship as an apparatus of government functions for domination of species by species and peoples by peoples by partitioning, individuating, and aggregating them into polities, it also opens possibilities of emancipation by producing the citizen subject capable of claiming 'I, we, they have a right to'. Can we name this citizen subject as revolutionary?

Revolutionary becoming and becoming revolutionary

If citizenship (in) acts always occurs in the fractures between citizenship (in) law and citizenship (in) practice, or between citizenship (in) theory and citizenship (in) practice, emancipatory possibilities present themselves. If citizenship (in) acts is irreducible to citizenship (in) practice because acts involve transforming polities, then can citizenship become revolutionary? If citizenship (in) acts reveals fractures between how citizenship (in) law regulates subjects of rights and how citizenship (in) practice provokes transformations, then when people capture its emancipatory potential, can citizenship become revolutionary? If citizenship (in) acts creates fractures that enable citizens and noncitizens to become counted for citizenship (in) law and when people seize emancipatory possibilities, can citizenship become revolutionary? If citizenship (in) acts can force emancipatory transformation in impenetrable polities, arrangements, or institutions, can we name it as revolutionary?

The answers to these questions will partially depend on how we signify revolutionary subjectivity. If we follow Arendt, who says that, before the age of revolutions, there were numerous revolts, rebellions, and uprisings but not revolutions, it would be difficult to signify citizenship as a revolutionary subjectivity without a revolution as an event that replaces one order with another or overturns one with another. Arendt thinks revolts, rebellions, and uprisings were not revolutionary because their claims were not radical enough to displace and overturn existing regimes. The subjects of these events were content with piecemeal changes. This is because, as strangers (paupers, women, black, indigenous) and outsiders (slaves, indentured, foreigners, alien), they imagined that their status in life was inherited or natural. By contrast, after the revolutions, making rights claims advanced an imaginary which enabled the strangers and outsiders (dispossessed, oppressed, and repressed) to claim they were placed under these conditions by apparatuses of domination and their demands were for emancipation from these apparatuses. Arendt's claims were always questionable: that until the age of revolutions people were not attuned to revolutionary change, and that revolutionary change is not piecemeal but wholesale. Arendt repeats conventional imaginaries on modern revolutions where a revolution implies discontinuity (one order replaces another, typically through whatever means necessary, violent or nonviolent) and overturning (a wholesale transformation rather than ruptures). We must question these assumptions as they are widely shared in diverse fields of modern political thinking and in various sites of thinking politically. Tracing premodern revolutions of various types (whether they were integrative or centralised or partial or wholesale) in terms of both their causes and consequences Said Amir Arjomand (2019) documents many counter-examples to Arendt's assumptions. There were acts with revolutionary effects before the age of revolutions, and these effects were not necessarily wholesale overthrowing of governments. Yet, revolution is still imagined, if not as displacement and overturning, at least as a spectacular event. As Thomas Nail (2012) deftly illustrates, revolutionary subjectivity has been resignified in the last 30 years. To shift our attitude toward revolutionary subjectivity we will once again turn to performativity with a further discussion of the concept of rupture as an analytics. We will make a distinction between (1) rupture as a concept to signify multiple forms of struggle ranging from everyday resistances, refusals, evasion, active or passive actions to revolts, uprisings, spectacles, and insurgences. We will designate this meaning as *revolutionary becoming*; (2) rupture as a concept to signify not a displacement or overturning of a regime but making claims to the whole of a polity by its parts as a condition of possibility of a revolution, resignifying its meaning and force. We will designate this as *becoming revolutionary*.

We will recall Deleuze once again to reflect on these two types of subjectivation: revolutionary becoming and becoming revolutionary. Although Deleuze may not have made this distinction, it will be important for developing an idea of revolutionary subjectivity. Deleuze suggests that political thinking about revolution as either an overturn or uprising conceals other nuanced and subtle possibilities. Deleuze says that political thinking about revolution as a rupture that takes apparatuses of government apart, reaggregates its parts, and deindividuates its indivisibles have far-reaching possibilities for revolutionary becoming of peoples and becoming revolutionaries (Deleuze and Parnet [1977] 2002, 144–45). When Deleuze insists that 'the question of a revolution has never been utopian spontaneity or reorganising apparatuses of the state' (145), he asks whether an organisation is possible which is not modelled on the apparatuses of the state and instead prefigures or reconfigures a polity to come. This political thinking is about documenting the fact that '*a new type of revolution is in the course of becoming possible*' (147, emphasis original). For Deleuze the question of the future of the revolution actually impedes the question of the revolutionary-becoming of peoples now and everywhere (147).

These two types of subjectivation – revolutionary becoming and becoming revolutionaries – are necessary for taking apparatuses of government apart and for prefiguring and reconfiguring polities differently. We have seen that citizenship as an apparatus of government provokes political and social struggles through which people make claims to belonging, identity, inclusion, exclusion, participation, influence, engagement, and so on. These claims often articulate into laws of citizenship and citizenship laws ranging from civil, political, and social rights to labour, sexual, cultural, environmental, consumer, and other rights in and across various sites of struggle. And citizenship (in) theory is one such site that calls forth its performers both as actors *and* spectators in these struggles. Especially when we are performing political thinking on citizenship, we are implicated both as actors and spectators in these struggles and over the meanings and functions of an apparatus that organizes, regulates, and distributes rights in and across modern polities. By documenting new types of revolution in the course of becoming possible and identifying both types of subjectivation – revolutionary becomings and becoming revolutionaries – we are participating in their prefiguration and reconfiguration.

Through various rituals, practices, routines, protocols, institutions, declarations, proclamations, and statements, the apparatus of citizenship makes citizens through invitations, interpellations, enforcement, law, norms, rules, and regulations that produce heterogeneous and complex assemblages of citizenship as political subjectivity. Through citations, repetitions, and iterations of those elements that constitute the apparatus, subjectivities are performatively taken up and are resignified to take the apparatus apart and possibly reassemble it.

Making rights claims against injustice

How can these make citizenship potentially a revolutionary subjectivity? If we want to see political subjectivity as creative, inventive, and autonomous ways of becoming citizens through relating to oneself and others and for transforming practices of domination to open possibilities of emancipation, can we see citizenship as a revolutionary subjectivity as a performative force that ruptures ways of doings things and throws citizenship as an apparatus into uncertainty, indeterminacy, and the unknown? Can we name citizenship as that political subjectivity which is becoming revolutionary? We will see below when discussing Austin that Bourdieu (1991) also reflected on how subjects emancipate themselves when taking apart their own partitioning, individuation, and aggregation. If what makes political subjectivity revolutionary is not only that it is creative, inventive, and autonomous but that it also articulates an injustice and claims its redress, how does this demand or claim can name revolutionary political subjectivity? These are the questions that acts of citizenship provoke. We place emphasis on the revolutionary acts that produce creative, inventive, and autonomous citizen subjects. If citizenship is performative, and there are those whose acts interrogate and transgress, can we name it a revolutionary subjectivity?

Citizenship as making rights claims means that before there are any rights there is the right to be political subjects and that the right to be political can only exist by being performed. Without performing that right (to have or claim rights), can we claim citizenship as a revolutionary subjectivity? To put it another way, and perhaps a counterintuitive way, we must become political subjects before we become claimants of any rights, however named and imagined. Without struggling as political subjects we cannot articulate ourselves into the languages of dignity, justice, peace, freedom, speech let alone economic, social, cultural, sexual, or nonhuman rights. We cannot claim our solidarity with other species and other peoples, however named and imagined. The sources of the right to become political subjects are performative and not given. It is social and political struggles that connect and combine demands and claims and articulate them through available sources (legal, illegal, social, cultural, religious, planetary, or other) through which we constitute ourselves and others as humans, peoples, and citizens.

This is where we can begin to see how making rights claims prefigures possibilities of both becoming revolutionary and revolutionary becoming by making citizenship sensible and intelligible as an apparatus of government. If we approach citizenship as an already given status, our concern would be things such as rules, regulations, and laws that govern who can and cannot be a citizen in a given polity. We would want to know who qualifies for citizenship and the laws of acquisition and deprivation of citizenship. We would consider things such as *jus sanguinis* (whereby a child inherits citizenship via a parent), *jus soli* (whereby a child inherits citizenship via birth regardless of parentage) or *jus domicili* (whereby an adult acquires citizenship by naturalisation in a polity other than that of their birth). We would think that these three principles (*jus sanguinis, jus soli,* and *jus domicili*) attach statuses to individual or collective bodies. Many scholars, especially in law but also in sociology and politics, focus on citizenship as status because it affects who can or cannot hold rights in a given polity. Approaching citizenship as status also includes consideration of the legal rights of citizens in a given polity. This is probably the most dominant way of approaching citizenship. We witness how national, international, supranational, and transnational rights in modern polities are rapidly changing struggles as these rights are articulated. We also witness how social rights (e.g., welfare benefits, housing subsidies, unemployment insurance) and civil liberties such as privacy, due process in courts, and rights to assembly pertain in a given polity and across polities.

If we approach citizenship as habitus we would be interested in how citizens and perhaps noncitizens practise the rights that they do have. Just because citizens have the right to vote, participate, claim benefits, move, and so on, this should not imply that they practise these rights, and we would be interested to know why they do and why they do not. Quite understandably, sociologists and anthropologists have contributed most to this approach to citizenship through studies of citizenship practices. Rather than attaching statuses to bodies, approaching citizenship as habitus asks how those bodies come into being and how those statuses get attached to them. That is why they have also been interested in things such as multicultural, sexual, global, and environmental forms of citizenship as these indicate different and sometimes perhaps novel ways of practising citizenship.

When we approach acts of citizenship, we see how people constitute themselves as political subjects by their performative utterances. By approaching citizenship as a revolutionary subjectivity, we see how peoples resist being partitioned into the people as a whole in terms that are articulated by dominant imaginaries. When we approach acts of citizenship, we see people transgress norms, expectations, routines, rituals, in short, their habitus. This transgression is revolutionary as it is the condition of possibility of making citizenship as an apparatus of government sensible and intelligible. And without transgressing citizenship as an apparatus of government there is no revolution – however understood. This is because if we approach citizenship as status, we focus on already constituted polities, as it were, under which those with status practise their citizenship or those without are denied from practising it. When we approach acts of citizenship, we see how those whose status is not citizenship may act as if it is and claim rights that they may not have. This is a rupture in a sense that makes citizenship as an apparatus of government for domination sensible and intelligible.

Rupture, revolt, revolution

To understand rupture better, we shall yet again return to Arendt. As we have seen, although she did not believe in premodern revolutionary subjectivity, her understanding of what makes revolutionary subjectivity is crucial for understanding how transgression of citizenship as an apparatus of government happens and how it can affect citizenship as a revolutionary subjectivity. This is relevant to considering subversion, disobedience, and dissent as beginning something new rather than reproducing habitus.

Arendt starts from the position that action – as distinguished from not only contemplation but also work and labour – enables human beings to perform their subjectivity, which involves bringing something new into the world whose outcomes are unpredictable. If humans were reproducible repetitions of the same whose essence was predictable, we would not need the concept of action (Arendt [1958] 1998, 8). Arendt differentiates action from practice and understands action as the beginning of something new. For Arendt each human shares the condition of natality, which cultivates the drive to initiate something new because we are born with the inherent capacity to come into the world as new ([1958] 1998, 9). Both speech and action or, more accurately, speech as action reveal this capacity and disclose each human being in the presence of and in relation to others ([1958] 1998, 176). Action as the disclosure of ourselves is something we can neither anticipate nor determine. Arendt reserves the term 'action' for the performance of this indeterminate capacity. To act then means to take initiative, to begin and to set something new in motion. Because humans are newcomers and beginners by virtue of birth, they are always prompted into action, into disclosing themselves to others. Arendt calls this capacity, or what it enables human beings to initiate, a 'miracle' – not because it is mystical but because it is unexpected and unpredicted, or in Arendt's own words, 'not because we superstitiously believe in miracles, but because human beings, whether or not they know it, as long as they can act, are capable of achieving, and constantly do achieve, the improbable and unpredictable' ([1955] 2005b, 114). Each human is capable of performing the unexpected, and it is only through this performance that each human being is able to disclose themselves as human. The fact that humans are capable of action means that the unexpected can be expected from them. We can perform what is currently unimaginable. This is possible because each human is endowed with this capacity. With each birth something uniquely new comes into the world (Arendt [1958] 1998, 177–8). What an action reveals or discloses is not a being that already exists but a being that emerges through this disclosure or revelation. That Arendt starts with this capacity does not mean that she implies a sovereign subject capable of commanding a will and controlling the outcomes of their actions. We shall see shortly how Arendt addresses this, but now let us take a step back and consider why it is important to consider the acting subject that places emphasis on this capacity to bring something new into the world.

Theorising action was so fundamental to Arendt that it concerned her throughout the 1950s and 1960s. We can trace the origins of this concern to the end of *Totalitarianism* (Arendt 1951). There, having traced the conditions that led to the rise of totalitarian regimes, she concludes that totalitarianism is distinctive and should not be equated with despotism, tyranny, or dictatorship. Then she ends her reflections with a passionate discussion of isolation, solitude, and loneliness. It may appear surprising to end a book on the origins of totalitarianism with existential concerns about solitude and loneliness, but this is precisely the point: that totalitarianism both produced and was made possible by a subject who could not act, or rather, whose capacity to act was impeded. Totalitarianism was dependent upon shaping citizenship as an apparatus of government whose primary mode of individuation was isolation through which people became separated, unable to act together. Their capacity to experience themselves as citizen subjects was repressed. What totalitarianism managed was to make people invest in its logic by withdrawing from what Arendt was already calling 'the great capacity of [people] to start something new' (1951, 473). Totalitarianism dominates people to make them invest in its logic, thus convincing them to surrender their capacity to begin something new. Arendt says, 'freedom as an inner capacity of [people] is identical with the capacity to begin, just as freedom as a political reality is identical with a space of movement between [peoples]' (1951, 473). Since power can only be exercised by acting together Arendt says isolated and atomised subjects become powerless. Totalitarianism destroys the capacity to act by subjecting people into isolation and atomisation. When subject citizens are isolated and atomised, they are captured in a situation where they cannot act because nobody will act with them. Arendt insists that isolation and loneliness are not the same. One can be lonely but still be in the company of others and, in fact, can act with others. By contrast, isolation is an 'impasse into which [people] are driven when the political sphere of their lives, where they act together in the pursuit of common concern, is destroyed' (Arendt 1951, 479). Arendt says while totalitarianism exacerbated isolation and atomisation these were already present in the origins and development of modern polities.

Arendt concludes that beginning, before it becomes a historical event, is our supreme capacity; it is freedom (1951, 479) Moreover, 'this beginning is guaranteed by each new birth; it is indeed every [person]' (Arendt [1958] 1998, 178). The disclosure of political subjectivity happens through words and deeds. For Arendt, without speech acts we would not only lose our revelatory character, but we would become automatons ([1958] 1998, 178).

Similarly, 'speechless action would no longer be action because there would no longer be an actor, and the actor, the doer of deeds, is possible only if [they are] at the same time the speaker of words' (Arendt [1958] 1998, 178–9). For Arendt the doer of deeds is not a sovereign subject with intentions and motives. She rejects the citizen subject who comes under the sway of either inner motives (subjectivism) or outer causes (objectivism) (Arendt 1961, 144). She accepts that 'although everybody started [their] life by inserting [themselves] into the human world through action and speech, nobody is the author or producer of [their] life story. In other words, the stories, the results of action and speech, reveal an agent, but this agent is not an author or producer' (Arendt [1958] 1998, 184). Arendt emphasises that we cannot know whom we reveal when we disclose ourselves in acts. The citizen subjects cannot explain themselves, but they can give reasons or accounts of themselves for their intentions, aims, and motives (Arendt [1958] 1998, 192). Since actions are inherently unpredictable and unknowable the effects can only be seen only when acts are performed. The full meaning of an act can only be produced when it has ended. We can see a powerful desire in Arendt to see political acts as emancipation from domination.

As we disclose ourselves to the world, our revolutionary subjectivity arises from acting together since we always disclose ourselves in the presence of others. We share our words and deeds (Arendt [1958] 1998, 197). What makes these words and deeds endure (Arendt [1958] 1998, 233)? Arendt identifies two qualities that can guarantee the endurance of acts: forgiving and promising ([1958] 1998, 237). Forgiveness ensures that people are able take risks in the face of the unpredictability of their actions by trusting those in whose presence they disclose themselves and in whose trust they place their disclosure. This requires courage (Arendt 1961, 156). It is this trust in the forgiveness of others that enables people to introduce themselves to the world. Thus, forgiveness itself is an act that 'does not merely re-act but acts anew and unexpectedly, unconditioned by the act which provoked it and therefore freeing from its consequences both the one who forgives and the one who is forgiven' (Arendt [1958] 1998, 241). Similarly, what protects people when taking risks is that people make and keep promises. This encourages us in the face of the unpredictability and uncertainty of our actions. Arendt emphatically states that forgiveness and promising build trust that is much stronger than any contract or treaty as the foundation of a body of citizens. The sovereignty of such a body politic, unlike that of 'we, the people' or the people as a whole, is not based on a unified will that inspires or coerces all its parts but an agreed purpose for which the promises are binding but can be broken. The point for Arendt is that the disclosure of ourselves through unpredictable and uncertain actions becomes our way of emancipating ourselves from domination not by a sovereign will but with a capacity to call something new into being whose outcome is unpredictable (2005a, 429). Arendt differentiates 'a freedom of choice that arbitrates and decides between two given things, one good and one evil, and whose choice is pre-determined by motive which has only to be argued to start its operation' from 'the freedom to call something into being which did not exist before, which was not given, not even as an object of cognition or imagination, and which therefore, strictly speaking, could not be known' (1961, 151). Thus, for Arendt people are emancipated as long as they act, neither before nor after because 'to be free and to act are the same' (1961, 153). For this reason, 'every act, seen from the perspective not of the agent but of the process in whose framework it occurs and whose automatism it interrupts, is a "miracle" that is, something which could not be expected' (Arendt 1961, 169). This is why Arendt actually speaks the freedom of the action rather than the actor.

Arendt says for action to be free it must be free from motives and aims. 'This is not to say that motives and aims are not important factors in every single act, but they are its determining factors, and action is free to the extent that it is able to transcend them' (1961, 151). Arendt insists that the goals, ends, and meanings of an action do not overlap and 'in the course of one and the same action they can end up at such logger-heads that the actors stumble into the gravest conflicts and the historians who follow after, whose task it is to accurately relate what in fact happened, can find themselves in endless debates over interpretation' [1955] 2005b, 198).

Arendt on action involves three elements: that the ends of an action cannot follow from the means it employs (actions exceed end–means calculability); that its goals cannot be attributed to either internal motives (subjectivism) or external causes (objectivism); and, that the meaning of an action is always contained within itself, and when an action ceases, that meaning ceases with the action itself.

Arendt says that 'in addition to these three elements of every political action – the end that it pursues, the goal which it has in mind and by which it orients itself, and the meaning that reveals itself in the course of the action' we must also add a fourth element [1955] 2005b, 194).

Arendt calls this fourth element the principle of action and describes it in 'psychological terms' as 'the fundamental conviction that a group of people share' ([1958] 1998, 152). For Arendt, action ultimately springs from its principles. The principle is too broad to have specific actions with goals anchored to it, although specific aims can be judged against it.

'For, unlike the judgment of the intellect which precedes action, and unlike the command of the will which initiates it, the inspiring principle becomes fully manifest only in the performing act itself' (Arendt [1958] 1998, 152) Unlike goals, motives and aims, 'the principle of an action can be repeated time and again, it is inexhaustible, and in distinction from its motive, the validity of a principle is universal, it is not bound to any particular person or to any particular group' (Arendt [1958] 1998, 152). Yet, the principles become manifest only through action and 'they are manifest in the world as long as the action lasts, but no longer' (Arendt [1958] 1998, 152).

Arendt is inspired by Montesquieu's ([1748] 1989) distinction between the letter and the spirit of the law. She says for Montesquieu this is the principle by which people in a polity act and are inspired to act (Arendt 1972, 94). When the letter and the spirit of the law come into conflict the letter must give way since the spirit of the law is an expression of nego-tiation and struggle over a lengthy period of time and provides, as Arendt says, the principle that inspires people to act. The right to dissent arises from upholding this distinction. Thus, dissent is the condition of possibility of the law as it upholds the spirit of the law even if the letter of the law suppresses it.

Can we see the capacity to dissent as rupture in given polities as political subjectivity? Seeing this capacity as historical rather than 'inherent' means recognising that we have developed this capacity as a result of at least 2,500 years, if not 6,000, of struggles, negotiations, enactments, performances, and imaginaries. Can we see it as a histori-cally developed capacity that is worth identifying, maintaining, and instituting for emancipation from domination?

The answer involves what people often say when making rights claims: justice as the principle of acts. Derrida understands justice very much like Arendt understands the spirit of the law: the principle by which people in or across polities act and are inspired to act as opposed to the letter of the law which they must obey. As Derrida states, 'justice is not the law. Justice is what gives us the impulse, the drive, or the movement to improve the law, that is, to deconstruct the law. Without a call for justice we would not have any interest in deconstructing the law' (in Caputo 1996, 16–17). We can speak about such things as 'acts of forgiveness', 'acts of promise', or 'acts of violence' because we have developed these imaginaries over long periods of time by acting under their principles. The same applies to 'acts of citizenship': throughout history people have subversively and disobediently have rendered citi-zenship as an apparatus of government sensible and intelligible by revealing its emancipatory possibilities. Thinking about citizenship as performance or enactment enjoins, follows, and departs from political thinking about citizenship as an apparatus of government and revealing its possibilities for emancipation from the injustice of domination that represses our capacities to act.

What comes after citizenship

About 30 years ago, Étienne Balibar (1991) gave the response 'the citizen' to Jean-Luc Nancy's question 'who comes after the subject?'. Thinking with Foucault, who focused on the transformation between ancient and modern subjectivity as a transformation from subjects to citizens, from the world of subjection to the birth of the citizen subject, Balibar wondered 'whether [citizen subject], like a face of sand at the edge of the sea, is about to be effaced with the next great sea change' (1991, 55). This is as a vital question now as it was when Balibar asked. We suppose the answer will be given by the acts of those who seek out lines of flight from this apparatus, with the possibilities it provides for becoming revolutionary citizens despite the obstacles it erects.

The most striking thing about citizenship as an apparatus of government is that it enables conventions to be ruptured, which is essential to emancipation, and yet its assemblage provokes domination. Or is it the other way around, that it enables domination yet provokes emancipation? When citizen subjects become revolutionary by making rights claims that they may not be authorised to make or to rights that may not even yet exist, what follows is an unpredictable and unknown politics of the performative.

How do we give an account of ourselves as capable of creative (deliberate yet spontaneous, mischievous yet serious, courageous yet not heroic), inventive (surprising yet predictable, illegal yet righteous, outrageous yet reasonable), and autonomous (individual yet collective, scripted yet experimental, unauthorised yet meaningful) acts? Or, thinking with Arendt, how do we give an account of our capacity to bring something new into the world whose outcomes are unpredictable? How do we account for ourselves as revolutionary subjects? Scholars such as Shoshana Felman ([1980] 2003), Judith Butler ([1997] 2021; 2015), and Eve Kosofsky Sedgwick (2003) were drawn to performativity and enactment for political thinking about these questions. These scholars are concerned with understanding how we become subjects in ways that reject both objectivist and subjectivist accounts of political performance. We are especially concerned about giving reasons why we think citizenship is a revolutionary subjectivity that we find over an exceptionally lengthy period of the organisation of polities, starting from at least 2,500 years ago, if not 6,000 years ago.

We have seen how Arendt powerfully sees our capacity to act as our capacity for emancipation from domination against repressive, oppressive, and unjust effects of citizenship as an apparatus of government. We will discuss now, once again, performativity as not only an analytical device to understand how citizenship as an apparatus of government makes citizens but also as a claim about citizenship as a revolutionary subjectivity that questions its partitioning, individuating, and aggregating machinations. The politics of the performative after Austin is such that it embodies revolutionary subjectivity as its principal effect.

The fascinating thing about Austin is that every distinction he introduces remains unstable and ambiguous and yet continues to stir the imagination. Take, for example, his key distinction between constative and performative utterances. He thought that while constative utterances describe (or at least attempt to describe) a state of affairs, performative utterances produce the state of affairs. Although nobody finds this distinction actually tenable (ironically, beginning with Austin himself), it continues to stir analytic discussion. As an utterance itself it embodies an ambiguity about whether it merely describes a state of affairs or brings about or performs it. But what is at stake with this distinction, and why did it prove so generative? It states what is obvious for us: that a statement gathers meaning only through the effects that it produces.

This applies equally to the distinctions Austin introduced later. The differences between locutionary acts that involve saying something, illocutionary acts that involve urging something and perlocutionary acts that involve bringing about further and separate actions. Similarly, the distinctions between originary and secondary acts, between felicitous and infelicitous acts, between conventional and unconventional acts, and between serious and non-serious acts were regularly expressed. Again, Austin himself found these distinctions 'troubling' (1962, 109). Still, the most creative aspects of doing things with words, as Austin envisaged, is the performative force of speech as acts. If we broaden the concept of speech from utterance to actions (through gestures, gatherings, assemblies, placements) and movements that also involve multiple bodies, then we have the makings of quite distinct objects of investigation – acts.

Pierre Bourdieu's main criticism was precisely Austin's exclusive focus on linguistic utterances as speech acts. Bourdieu argues that social acts can succeed only when someone or something endowed with a specific status or property is backed by a group or institution. Acts as diverse as marriage or circumcision or conferment or attribution would never acquire their performative force without social conditions that make such acts recognizable and legitimate. This is the case even when an act is accomplished by a sole agent who still acts within recognised forms and according to certain conventions. Following Austin, those who interpret such acts as though the words used in them possess the performative force to accomplish them fail to appreciate that they are fundamentally social acts in the sense of being instituted and instituting social and political apparatuses. There is no illocutionary force without the words, but there are no words without apparatuses. For Bourdieu social acts generate their force, illocutionary and perlocutionary force if you like, not from linguistic forms that govern them but from social conditions that make them possible and the apparatuses that govern them. What renders an actor capable of accomplishing an act is precisely the collective belief that guarantees its institution (Bourdieu 1991, 125–6).

To put it differently, the illocutionary force of words cannot be found within those words themselves. The authority that gives words their performative force comes from outside those words themselves. For Bourdieu, what language performs is to represent this authority, manifest it, and symbolise it. The use of language depends on the social position of the speaker that governs the rules of legitimate speech (Bourdieu 1991, 109). What makes a speech legitimate is the symbolic power accumulated by the social group or institution that delegates the speaker. That is why the success of a performative utterance depends on the appropriateness of the speaker or their social function as a delegate. A performative utterance would fail if the speaker lacked such capacity or delegation to invest words with the power of his social function. In that sense, all speech acts are social acts, and all social acts are acts of authority. For a speech act to accomplish its performative force it does not need to be understood at all; it only needs to be recognised. For such a recognition to register, the speaker must show that they do not act in their own name and on their own authority but in their capacity as a delegate.

Although Bourdieu's intervention is powerful here in highlighting the fact that performative force is not inherent in words, he does not acknowledge that the success of a performative utterance can also depend on the *inappropriateness* of the speaker or their *lack* of social function as a delegate. Perhaps here the difference between focusing on conduct and on action becomes clearer. Bourdieu's concern is to give an account of the conduct of agents. But citizen subjects who act are often, if not always, in breach of the conventions that govern their conduct – dissent. What theorising acts concerns is giving an account, or at least developing an analytics, for understanding acts when subjects *fail* or *refuse* to follow conventions. Bourdieu's reminder that the performative force of words cannot be found within those words themselves is important. However, his insistence that the authority that gives words their performative force comes from outside those words themselves is not especially useful, principally because it seeks to identify the conditions of the possibility of conduct. Instead, we want to understand the conditions of the *impossibility* of conducting ourselves properly as the conditions of citizenship as a revolutionary subjectivity. This leads to another related but a distinct issue about originary versus mimetic acts.

The most significant aspect of discussion on performativity concerns whether the essence of a speech act is originary or citational or iterative. The issue here is to determine whether an act merely repeats an already existing repertoire, albeit under different conditions, or brings something 'creative, inventive, and autonomous' into the world (or, as Arendt would say, brings something new into the world with surprising effects). If the former is the case, then what is the point of calling something an act rather than a performance or practice? What is at stake here is more than the linguistic apparatus. It concerns one of the most troubling matters in political thinking about political subjectivity: as subjects how do we act creatively, inventively, and autonomously rather than imitatively, routinely, and dependently? If we become subjects by taking up scripts, routines, and conventions in life as given, inhabiting ways of being that have been scripted for us, then what is the promise of being creative, inventive, and autonomous? What are we bringing that is new to the world? Why are creativity, inventiveness, and autonomy conditions of possibility of revolutionary subjectivity? Why insist on our capacity to bring something new to the world with a surprising outcome? For revolutionary subjectivity, it is essential to have these attributes, for without them, we cannot imagine citizen subjects capable of enacting themselves as equal, critical, and activist subjects who will discriminate between justice and injustice, between equal and unequal and between right and wrong. Admittedly, if we understand citizenship as political subjectivity it is because we already hold an idea of subjectivity involving creativity, inventiveness, and autonomy. If that subject we call a citizen always acts within given scripts, how do we account for the change in our understanding of citizenship as an apparatus of government?

We have been persistently using a term, rupture, to describe what happens when citationality and iterability exceed their possibilities, reveal their vulnerabilities, and open up opportunities for subversion – acting otherwise or cracking the apparatus. Acts can cite, iterate, and repeat, but they can also do so differently and not necessarily as more of the same. But how do we know when an act is resignification rather than iteration or repetition? We need to return to the idea of rupture one last time.

Both Rancière and Laclau describe the moment when politics arises as a rupture. For Rancière politics is a rupture of the dominant order. Rancière says 'politics does not happen just because the poor oppose the rich. It is the other way around: politics (that is, the interruption of the simple effects of domination by the rich) causes the poor to exist as an entity' ([1995] 1998, 11). Similarly, Laclau believes that the moment that we inhabit is one that will require ruptures through acts that will have aggregating effects on politics (2005, 230). Laclau uses derivative versus constitutive to define rupture. He says, for example, the birth of a people as an historical actor creates a configuration that is not derivative but constitutive (2005, 228). But in what sense can we differentiate derivative from constitutive? The birth of a people 'constitutes an act in the strict sense, for it does not have its source in anything external to itself' (Laclau 2005, 228). Laclau also uses words such as transgressive and subversive to define rupture. This transgression is an act that does not simply replace existing order but introduces a different order (Laclau 2005, 229). This is 'because the act, on the one hand, brings about a new (ontic) order, but, on the other, has an ordering (ontological) function, it is the locus of a complex game by which a concrete content actualises, through its very concreteness, something that is entirely different from itself' (Laclau 2005, 229). Yet, this is a revolutionary act only insofar as it cannot describe itself in advance as an overtaking or replacement of an order. For a rupture to be transgression or subversion, it cannot name in advance its own effects but introduces rupture in a given order (Laclau 2005, 237).

Still, for both Rancière and Laclau, the concept of rupture (and its relation to acts) remains elusive. Laclau identifies his concept of the act with that of Lacan's 'passage to the act', but this is confusing, as we shall see later. Similarly, we find the idea of rupture as the essence of politics in Badiou when he says 'all resistance is a rupture with what is. And every rupture begins, for those engaged in it, through a rupture with oneself' (Badiou 2006, 24). Badiou insists that 'the essence of politics is not the plurality of opinions. It is the prescription of a possibility in rupture with what exists' (Badiou 2006, 24). He suggests that what accomplishes these ruptures are declarations, interventions, and organisations. Yet, Badiou does not relate rupture to acts let alone consider rupture as the essence of acts. Instead, Badiou considers something an act only if it is revolutionary in the sense of bringing about a radical overturn.

Derrida too struggles with the idea of rupture. He identifies the force of performativity with rupture. In many ways, he becomes critical of speech acts as exemplified especially by Austin and Searle primarily on this point. For Derrida, the originary performativity that does not conform to preexisting conventions, unlike all the performatives analyzed by the theoreticians of speech acts, but whose force of *rupture* produces the institution or the constitution, the law itself, which is to say also the meaning that appears to, that ought to, or that appears to have to guarantee it in return.

([1993] 1994, 36–7)

Contrasting performativity with performance (citational, repetitive, iterative) Derrida thinks that if an iterative event intervenes in performativity, it is always accidental and not intrinsic to it ([2000] 2002, 224).

For Butler, what is politically significant about rupture is 'the moment in which a subject – a person, a collective – asserts a right or entitlement to a liveable life when no such prior authorisation exists, when no clearly enabling convention is in place' (2004, 224). To put it differently, for Butler, the force of performativity is its creativity as far as an act is 'not inherited from prior usage, but issues forth precisely from its break with any and all prior usage. That break, that force of rupture, is the force of the performative' ([1997] 2021, 149). Still, what exactly does it mean to say or do something that will not inherit its force from prior usage but break with it? This is where a rupture and an event become conflated. We can provisionally suggest that what reveals an act as a rupture is the event that the act produces. As Derrida says, 'wherever there is some performative, that is, in the strict and Austinian sense of the term, the mastery in the first person present of an "I can," "I may" guaranteed and legitimated by conventions, well, then, all pure eventness is neutralised, muffled, suspended' ([2000] 2002, 239). By contrast, if we claim that 'I, we, they, have a right to ...' we are enacting citizenship as a revolutionary subjectivity in its unpredictability, unknowability, and instability. If indeed such performative acts produce the event of which they speak, it is this aspect that transforms a performative utterance into an act without not without prior convention but in cracking it.

If the concept of rupture proved challenging, it is for good reason. If and when we consider politics as the interruption or disruption against domination and for tracing lines of flight as emancipation, citizenship as an apparatus of government moves centre stage as it involves making the citizen subject the smallest indivisible part of politics and involves how its parts combine with other parts to create and maintain its apparatus. What is evocative about using rupture is its performativity: it gains meaning only when it is demonstrated or illustrated – performed. The scandal of citizenship as a revolutionary subjectivity arises when subjects without history make their way into citizenship as an apparatus of government, transform its partitions, subvert its individuations, and take apart its aggregations, and become citizen subjects through lines of flight as unpredictable, unknowable, and unstable claims against domination for emancipation.

Conclusion
Planetary citizenship?

Over 6,000 years our species invented polities (cities, states, empires) by assembling apparatuses for governing multiplicities as peoples, partitioning, individuating, and aggregating them into insiders (citizens) and outsiders (strangers, aliens, foreigners). Although a fraction of the 200,000-year history of our species, and its settlement of Planet Earth that began about 100,000 years ago, these 6,000 thousand years accelerated, intensified, and transformed our species and other species by constituting them and ourselves as objects of domination. That we have now named its recent history or any of its more recent episodes (e.g., 75, 200, 500, 2,500, or 6,000 years ago) as the domination of Planet Earth by our species – Anthropocene – signals that at least we have become aware of the consequences of our effects on the planet. Whether, and if so how, we can sustain it as our common habitat are now planetary questions.

As Dipesh Chakrabarty (2021) argues, these planetary questions force our species to imagine ourselves as inhabitants of Planet Earth, sharing a common habitat with other species. This, Chakrabarty says, should make it now possible to see the world history of the last 6,000 years, where our species has dominated, in relation to earth history that stretches back at least 200,000 years, with the beginning of our species and much beyond. Scholars such as Shryock and Smail (2011), Gamble (2013), and Krause and Trappe (2022) have expanded our imaginaries beyond the dominant histories where our species and Euro-American peoples in particular appear as triumphant victors against sedentary, ancient, eastern, and nonhuman worlds. As Jerry Bentley (2011) argues the task of world history has become complicated with the appearance of earth history. We are now beginning to see the transformations of polities 6,000 years ago against a larger canvas of world history considering artefact, symbolic, genetic, and digital archives together. The history before our species is still considered as 'prehistory', but the separation between earth history and world history is weakening, and the idea of prehistory is waning.

DOI: 10.4324/9781003395997-6

If indeed the earth is becoming uninhabitable through the activities of our species, when this started and whether it can be averted has become not only the concern of sciences, but it has become a concern for arts, philosophy, and religion where film, fiction and science-fiction, poetry, photography, painting, dance, theatre, and music respond to and participate in the production of a planetary imaginary. Various religions ranging from Buddhism to Taoism if not Islam, Judaism, and Christianity have also been forced to reflect on the present predicament of Planet Earth as a habitat of both human and nonhuman species. The planetary imaginary now involves the formation of numerous movements for climate justice connecting it with movements for racial, gender, and social justice. This is not to say the planetary imaginary is coherent or unified. On the contrary, it is the object of struggles to shape, name, organise, and define it by interpellating or inviting people into embodying its concerns. The planetary imaginary is not ideology, fantasy, imagination, utopia or dystopia – it is all of these, but it traverses them in its dispersion, dissemination, uptake, and interpellation and it is not reducible to any one or any combination of them.

Are we then *not* seeing the emergence of a planetary citizenship as an apparatus of government? This question places our species in a predicament for intraspecies and interspecies solidarities as, being the species having now had the decisive impact on this common habitat, the planetary imaginary is not about ourselves alone but about Planet Earth as the common habitat of all planetary species.

Gianfranco Pellegrino (2022) proposes a concept of ecological citizenship where nonhuman subjects enter into history as political subjects. Are we witnessing the birth of planetary citizens? Perhaps, but, as we have seen, there are dangers in the progressive inclusion of nonhuman species in citizenship as an apparatus of government without understanding how its fractures and lines assemble this apparatus. As Alfred (1999) and Simpson (2014) show, an inclusion in the terms articulated by domination does not lead to emancipation. Can planetary citizens become revolutionary citizens?

We must recognise that our species' domination of other species has not only involved interspecies but also intraspecies domination. The inventions of god-kings, slavery, bondage, servitude, and cruelty were early evidence of the domestication of the human species – homo domesticus. These inventions as both affects and effects provoked our species to partition ourselves into classes, races, sexes, and religions, individuate ourselves into black, white, man, woman, abled, disabled, and aggregate ourselves into various warring peoples, states, nations, and corporations. What we are beginning to recognise that the history of domestication of Planet Earth by our species will not be understood without its associated domestication of ourselves through cities, states, and empires as organised polities with their apparatuses of government. Emancipation struggles against domination were present as long ago as when these inventions subjected peoples and species to domination. Yet, these polities also enabled resistance and defiance to be articulated as acts of emancipation from domination. The birth of the citizen subject is the event that most powerfully enacts this.

Those engaged in political thinking are attuned to these developments with their attention to deep history. We have already seen how James Scott (2017) questions the dominant histories and overturns the origins of cities, states, and empires from the perspective of barbarians. Similarly, scholars such as Antony Black ([2009] 2016) and Peter Clark (2013) have produced work on political thinking and polities with much larger canvases of world history.

Given this shift in perspectives on world history and earth history of political thinking and thinking politically about polities, as Anthropocene in both its affect and effect, citizenship as a concept cannot survive in its dominant form as an institution either of nation or state or as membership or status and the citizen subject as proprietor, legislator, magistrate, selector, and soldier. We have now written new citizen subjects into history. A recent and outstanding collection of essays, for example, on antiquity and citizenship write new citizen subjects into histories of citizenship in Greek and Roman polities and even earlier polities in Anatolia, Mesopotamia, and Africa (Filonik, Plastow, and Zelnick-Abramovitz 2023). Alain Duplouy (2023) argues, for example, in both archaic and classical Greece, citizenship not only featured diverse performative repertoires beyond the citizen subject as proprietor, legislator, magistrate, selector, and soldier, but it also spawned diverse ordinary languages. Duplouy (2018) had already captured this diversity as citizenship as performance in ancient Greek polities. Similarly, Ellen Meiksins Wood (1997; 2008) and Josine Blok (2017) write peasants and women into the history of classical Greek citizenship. We now have imaginaries of diverse citizen subjects playing with citizenship as an apparatus of government through their acts of emancipation in law, justice, and citizenship whether it is in Plato's Athens (Prauscello 2014) or Shakespeare's London (Archer 2005). Maarten Prak (2018) discusses diverse acts of emancipation in European and non-European cities in the last 1,000 years in a provocative history and writes new citizen subjects into history.

There are many more examples of how, over the last 30 years, a revolutionary concept of citizenship has been developed by activists, artists, scholars, and scientists writing subjects without history (e.g., animals, children, gays, indigenous peoples, lesbians, migrants, minorities, mothers, mountains, paupers, plants, prisoners, protesters, refugees, rivers, robots, slaves, transgender peoples, trees, women, and workers) into both world history and earth history. This book hopefully sharpens our sense of how all this is connected with citizenship as an apparatus of government.

Although sporadically, precariously, and fleetingly, as citizenship became the name of acts of emancipation in the last 2,500 years, we certainly have evidence of such acts before, or without being named as, citizenship. Yet, the naming of citizenship 2,500 years ago had revolutionary effects. This originary event as the naming of the citizen subject – an emancipated subject – being able to govern themselves and others as autonomous subjects has been repeated, reiterated, cited, resignified, and transformed ever since either as claims or counterclaims.

The originary event has been an effect and not a cause of citizenship as an apparatus of government. Yet, as soon as the naming of the citizen subject announces an emancipated subject, it already institutes various forms of domination of other peoples and species by partitioning, individuating, and aggregating them into hierarchies. The naming of the citizen subject from its originary event onward is fractured. We identified these with lines of movement, technology, coloniality, sovereignty, and planetarity. Citizenship as an apparatus of government depended on the fractures that these lines reveal: between sedentary and nomadic, episteme and techne, east and west, ancient and modern, and human and nonhuman. We argued that these were not opposites but fractures that precariously assemble citizenship as an apparatus.

These fractures continue to shape political thinking and thinking politically about citizenship as its difference machines rather than opposites. Thinking about these fractures as difference machines provides a revolutionary perspective on citizenship as an apparatus of government. The oppositions between nomadic and sedentary subjects conceal how these modes of subjectivity are implicated in and traverse each other. It is necessary to understand how citizenship as an apparatus of government functions through movement rendering certain movements legitimate and others illegitimate. We have seen how technology implicates both techne and episteme in each other for partitioning, individuating, and aggregating peoples by developing both devices and protocols for making peoples and things. The invention of the corporation as a juridical-political-economic technology becomes central to citizenship as an apparatus of government. We have also seen how coloniality partitions spaces into superior and inferior, capable and incapable, backward and forward by occupying lifeworlds in these spaces. Citizenship as an apparatus of government partitions time by constituting itself as the originary (modern) moment and disavows its past as ancient. The naming of the citizen subject declares itself as an originary emancipation from domination as it institutes new forms of domination including the domination of other species as nonhuman subjects. And now the naming of the citizen as a human subject comes apart by partitioning itself from Planet Earth as both its tormentor and saviour, individuating nonhuman species, and aggregating them into anthropomorphised humanoids and androids.

A concept of citizenship as an apparatus of government from this history is necessary, not because we bring all sorts of things together under this concept across history, but rather because we identify variations that make it a sensible and intelligible object. Citizenship is inevitably tangled with other concepts such as noncitizenship, strangers, outsiders, foreigners, aliens, peoples, the people, and more apparatuses in different sites and senses of enactment. But each site and sense of enactment of this apparatus mobilises heterogenous and variable elements. Another way of saying this is that citizenship as an apparatus of government stays the same in its name but constantly mutates in its functions. To accomplish this difficult task of identifying that which stays the same to understand that which constantly changes we have proposed investigating the cracks and fractures that precariously assemble citizenship as an apparatus of government (Chapter 1), the sites of enactment through which the apparatus is assembled (Chapter 2), the ways in which the apparatus is rendered sensible and intelligible (Chapter 3), and how it produces a revolutionary subjectivity (Chapter 4). We have enveloped these chapters with an introduction that provides reasons and methods for studying citizenship as an apparatus of government and the present conclusion on what is at stake with studying citizenship.

As citizenship as an apparatus of government precariously traverses the assemblages of other apparatuses of government such as security, territory, health, and wealth these fractures reveal its lines of visibility, utterance, subjectivity, and flight. We can see these lines in how citizenship as an apparatus of government is assembled in law, theory, practice, and acts. Both political thinking and thinking politically traverse these sites. Laws of citizenship partition peoples into citizens and noncitizens, citizenship laws individuate both citizens and noncitizens into modes of conduct and being, and laws of citizenship again aggregate them as peoples. Citizenship (in) law conceals citizenship as an apparatus of government by narrowing its scope to insiders and thus drawing a line between insiders and outsiders and by dispersing or fragmenting insiders across several other apparatuses of government as diverse fields of law. We cannot emphasise enough the importance of this distinction. By concealing citizenship as an apparatus of government citizenship laws isolate and atomise people so much so that they never experience their struggles over citizenship as such. Another way of saying this is that citizenship as an apparatus of government succeeds as far as it makes itself appear as ordinary rather than a revolutionary subjectivity. Thus, it is necessary to deconstruct the ordinary language of citizenship.

Citizenship (in) theory also conceals citizenship as an apparatus of government by political thinking that idealises, normalises, idolises citizenship while thinking politically focuses on atomised and isolated rights associated with the claims of partitioned peoples. Citizenship theory as political thinking creates its own series and makes its author-function appear independent and outside of citizenship as an apparatus of government by providing insider insights. Citizenship theory as political thinking becomes incommensurable with thinking politically about citizenship and can never suture the fracture between several apparatuses of government fragmented into different domains. Citizenship (in) practice is traversed by a line between citizenship practices that discipline, manage, regulate, and influence citizen conduct often supported by citizenship (in) theory as political thinking that idolises it and citizenship practices that repeatedly invent lines of flight that subvert and expose disciplinary practices. Acts *on* citizenship codify both meanings and functions of citizenship while acts *of* citizenship rupture the narratives and scripts of its codification.

Acts of citizenship are crucial for revealing or exposing citizenship as an apparatus of government and its fractures. Acts of citizenship produce a revolutionary subjectivity by making citizenship as an apparatus of government both sensible and intelligible. This means provoking social struggles over whose language is citizenship, questioning the partition between citizens and noncitizens, making rights claims where such rights may or may not already exist in laws of citizenship, creating instability when stability is commanded by keeping citizenship as an apparatus of struggle, and traversing lines that partition peoples and establishing solidarities, affinities, and connections amongst various struggles as struggles over citizenship.

This makes citizenship a revolutionary subjectivity if we understand revolutionary becoming and becoming revolutionary as acts of emancipation rather than complete or spontaneous takeovers of apparatuses of government. The last 6,000 year history of polities, especially the last 2,500 year history of citizenship as an apparatus of government, includes major uprisings, revolts, protests, rebellions, and revolutions, but minor ruptures that expose the fractures of citizenship as an apparatus of government (partitioning ourselves into classes, races, sexes, and religions, individuating ourselves into black, white, man, woman, abled, disabled, native, non-native, guest, host, and aggregating ourselves into various warring peoples, states, nations, and corporations) that have arguably made them possible.

Bibliography

Agamben, Giorgio. (1996) 2000. *Means Without End: Notes on Politics*. Translated by Vincenzo Binetti. Minnesota: University of Minnesota Press.

Agamben, Giorgio. (2006) 2009. *What Is an Apparatus? And Other Essays*. Translated by David Kishik and Stefan Pedatella. Stanford, CA: Stanford University Press.

Alfred, Taiaiake. 1999. *Peace, Power, Righteousness: An Indigenous Manifesto*. Oxford: Oxford University Press.

Alfred, Taiaiake, and Jeff Corntassel. 2005. 'Being Indigenous: Resurgences against Contemporary Colonialism'. *Government and Opposition* 40 (4): 597–614.

Anderson, Bridget, and Vanessa Hughes, eds. 2015. *Citizenship and Its Others*. London: Palgrave.

Archer, John Michael. 2005. *Citizen Shakespeare: Freemen and Aliens in the Language of the Plays*. Basingstoke: Palgrave Macmillan.

Arendt, Hannah. 1951. *The Origins of Totalitarianism*. 2nd ed. New York: Harcourt Brace Jovanovich.

Arendt, Hannah. (1958) 1998. *The Human Condition*. Chicago: University of Chicago Press.

Arendt, Hannah. 1961. *Between Past and Future: Six Exercises in Political Thought*. New York: Viking Press.

Arendt, Hannah. (1963) 1990. *On Revolution*. London: Penguin.

Arendt, Hannah. 1972. *The Crises of the Republic*. New York: Harcourt Brace Jovanovich.

Arendt, Hannah. 2005a. *Essays in Understanding, 1930–1954: Formation, Exile, and Totalitarianism*. New York: Schocken Books.

Arendt, Hannah. (1955) 2005b. 'Introduction into Politics'. In *The Promise of Politics*, edited by Jerome Kohn, 93–200. New York: Schocken Books.

Arjomand, Saïd Amir. 2019. *Revolution: Structure and Meaning in World History*. Chicago: University of Chicago Press.

Arneil, Barbara. 2007. 'Global Citizenship and Empire'. *Citizenship Studies* 11 (3): 301–328.

Austin, J.L. 1962. *How to Do Things with Words*. Oxford: Oxford University Press.

Austin, J.L. 1970. *Philosophical Papers*. Edited by J.O. Urmson and G.J. Warnock. 2nd ed. Oxford: Oxford University Press.

Badiou, Alain. 2006. *Metapolitics*. Translated by J. Barker. London: Verso.

Balibar, Étienne. 1991. 'Citizen Subject'. In *Who Comes after the Subject?*, edited by Eduardo Cadava, Peter Connor, and Jean-Luc Nancy, 33–57. London: Routledge.

Balibar, Étienne. (2011) 2017. *Citizen Subject: Foundations for Philosophical Anthropology*. Translated by Steven Miller. New York: Fordham University Press.

Balibar, Étienne. 2012. *Citizenship*. Translated by Thomas Scott-Railton. Cambridge: Polity.

Bauböck, Rainer. 2010. 'Studying Citizenship Constellations'. *Journal of Ethnic and Migration Studies* 36 (5): 847–859.

Beaney, Michael. 2012. 'Ordinary Language Philosophy'. In *Philosophy of Language*, edited by Delia Graff Fara and Gillian Russell, 873–884. London: Routledge.

Bentley, Jerry H. 2011. 'The Task of World History'. In *The Oxford Handbook of World History*, edited by Jerry H. Bentley. Oxford: Oxford University Press.

Berger, Stefan, and Holger Nehring, eds. 2017. *The History of Social Movements in Global Perspective: A Survey*. London: Palgrave Macmillan.

Berman, Harold J. 1983. *Law and Revolution: The Formation of Western Legal Tradition*. Cambridge, MA: Harvard University Press.

Bhambra, Gurminder K. 2015. 'Citizens and Others'. *Alternatives: Global, Local, Political* 40 (2): 102–114.

Bjork-James, Carwil, Melissa Checker, and Marc Edelman. 2022. 'Transnational Social Movements: Environmentalist, Indigenous, and Agrarian Visions for Planetary Futures'. *Annual Review of Environment and Resources* 47 (1): 583–608.

Black, Antony. (2009) 2016. *A World History of Ancient Political Thought: Its Significance and Consequences*. 2nd ed. Oxford: Oxford University Press.

Blok, Josine. 2017. *Citizenship in Classical Athens*. Cambridge: Cambridge University Press.

Bloom, Tendayi. 2017. *Noncitizenism: Recognising Noncitizen Capabilities in a World of Citizens*. London: Routledge.

Bourdieu, Pierre. (1980) 1990. *The Logic of Practice*. Translated by Richard Rice. Stanford, CA: Stanford University Press.

Bourdieu, Pierre. 1991. *Language and Symbolic Power*. Cambridge, MA: Harvard University Press.

Bowen, H.V. 2006. *The Business of Empire: The East India Company and Imperial Britain, 1756–1833*. Cambridge: Cambridge University Press.

Brandzel, Amy L. 2016. *Against Citizenship: The Violence of the Normative*. Dissident Feminisms. Urbana, Illinois: University of Illinois Press.

Butler, Judith. 1990. *Gender Trouble: Feminism and the Subversion of Identity*. London: Routledge.

Butler, Judith. 1993. *Bodies That Matter: On the Discursive Limits of 'Sex'*. London: Routledge.

Butler, Judith. (1997) 2021. *Excitable Speech: A Politics of the Performative*. 2nd ed. London: Routledge.

Butler, Judith. 2004. *Undoing Gender*. London: Routledge.

Butler, Judith. 2015. *Notes Toward a Performative Theory of Assembly.* Cambridge: Harvard University Press.

Byrd, Jodi A. 2011. *The Transit of Empire: Indigenous Critiques of Colonialism.* Minneapolis: University of Minnesota Press.

Canning, Joseph P. 1980. 'The Corporation in the Thought of Thirteenth and Fourteenth Jurists'. *History of Political Thought* 1 (1): 9–32.

Canovan, Margaret. 2005. *The People.* Cambridge: Polity.

Caputo, John D., ed. 1996. *Deconstruction in a Nutshell: A Conversation with Jacques Derrida.* Perspectives in Continental Philosophy, No. 1. New York: Fordham University Press.

Castoriadis, Cornelius. (1975) 1987. *The Imaginary Institution of Society.* Translated by Kathleen Blamey. French Edition (1975). Cambridge: Polity.

Cavell, Stanley. (1969) 1976. *Must We Mean What We Say?*2nd ed. Cambridge: Cambridge University Press.

Cavell, Stanley. (1979) 1999. *The Claim of Reason: Wittgenstein, Skepticism, Morality, and Tragedy.* 2nd ed. Oxford: Oxford University Press.

Cavell, Stanley. 1994. *A Pitch of Philosophy: Autobiographical Exercises.* Cambridge, Mass.: Harvard University Press.

Chakrabarty, Dipesh. 2021. *The Climate of History in a Planetary Age.* Chicago: University of Chicago Press.

Clark, Peter, ed. 2013. *The Oxford Handbook of Cities in World History.* Oxford Handbooks in History. Oxford: Oxford University Press.

Cohen, Elizabeth F. 2009. *Semi-Citizenship in Democratic Politics.* Cambridge: Cambridge University Press.

Connolly, William E. 2017. *Facing the Planetary: Entangled Humanism and the Politics of Swarming.* Durham: Duke University Press.

Couture, Selena. 2014. 'Performativity of Time, Movement and Voice in Idle No More'. *Performance Research* 19 (6): 118–120.

Croix, G.E.M. Ste de. 1993. *The Class Struggle in the Ancient Greek World: From the Archaic Age to the Arab Conquests.* Ithaca, NY: Cornell University Press.

Dalrymple, William. 2019. *The Anarchy: The Relentless Rise of the East India Company.* London: Bloomsbury.

Dassow, Eva von. 2023. 'Citizens and Non-Citizens in the Age of Hammurabi'. In *Citizenship in Antiquity: Civic Communities in the Ancient Mediterranean,* edited by Jakub Filonik, Christine Plastow, and Rachel Zelnick-Abramovitz, 81–97. London: Routledge.

Deleuze, Gilles. (1980) 1995. *Negotiations, 1972–1990.* New York: Columbia University Press.

Deleuze, Gilles. (1986) 1988. *Foucault.* Translated by Seán Hand. Minneapolis: University of Minnesota Press.

Deleuze, Gilles. (1989) 2006. 'What Is Dispositif?' In *Two Regimes of Madness: Texts and Interviews 1975–1995,* translated by David Lapoujade and Michael Taormina, 338–348. New York: Semiotext[e].

Deleuze, Gilles. (1990a) 1995. 'Control and Becoming'. In *Negotiations, 1972–1990,* translated by Martin Joughin, 169–176. New York: Columbia University Press.

Deleuze, Gilles. (1990b) 1995. 'PostScript on Control Societies'. In *Negotiations, 1972–1990*, translated by Martin Joughin, 177–182. New York: Columbia University Press.

Deleuze, Gilles, and Felix Guattari. (1980) 1987. *A Thousand Plateaus: Capitalism and Schizophrenia*. Translated by Brian Massumi. Minneapolis: University of Minnesota Press.

Deleuze, Gilles, and Claire Parnet. (1977) 2002. *Dialogues II*. Translated by Tomlinson, Hugh, Habberjam, Barbara, and Eliot Ross Albert. New York: Columbia University Press.

Derrida, Jacques. (1967) 1978. *Writing and Difference*. Translated by Alan Bass. London: Routledge.

Derrida, Jacques. (1977) 1988. *Limited Inc*. Edited by Gerald Graff. Evanston, Illinois: Northwestern University Press.

Derrida, Jacques. 1986. 'Declarations of Independence'. *New Political Science 7* (1): 7–15.

Derrida, Jacques. (1993) 1994. *Specters of Marx: State of the Debt, the Work of Mourning and the New International*. Translated by Peggy Kamuf. London: Routledge.

Derrida, Jacques. (2000) 2002. *Without Alibi*. Translated by Peggy Kamuf. Stanford, CA: Stanford University Press.

Du Bois, W. E. B. (1935) 2013. *Black Reconstruction in America: Toward a History of the Part Which Black Folk Played in the Attempt to Reconstruct Democracy in America, 1860–1880*. Edited by Mack H. Jones. London: Transaction Publishers.

Duplouy, Alain. 2018. 'Citizenship as Performance'. In *Defining Citizenship in Archaic Greece*, edited by Alain Duplouy and Roger Brock, 249–274. Oxford: Oxford University Press.

Duplouy, Alain. 2023. 'Lifestyle and Behaviour in Archaic and Classical Greece: The Other Language of Citizenship'. In *Citizenship in Antiquity: Civic Communities in the Ancient Mediterranean*, edited by Jakub Filonik, Christine Plastow, and Rachel Zelnick-Abramovitz, 48–63. London: Routledge.

Elden, Stuart. 2016. *Foucault's Last Decade*. Cambridge: Polity.

Emberling, Geoff, Sarah C. Clayton, and John W. Janusek. 2015. 'Urban Landscapes: Transforming Spaces and Reshaping Communities'. In *Early Cities in Comparative Perspective, 4000 BCE-1200 CE*, edited by Norman Yoffee, 3:300–316. The Cambridge World History. Cambridge: Cambridge University Press.

Fahrmeir, Andreas. 2008. *Citizenship: The Rise and Fall of a Modern Concept*. New Haven: Yale University Press.

Felman, Shoshana. (1980) 2003. *The Scandal of the Speaking Body: Don Juan with J. L. Austin, or Seduction in Two Languages*. Translated by Catherine Porter. Stanford, CA: Stanford University Press.

Filonik, Jakub, Christine Plastow, and Rachel Zelnick-Abramovitz, eds. 2023. *Citizenship in Antiquity: Civic Communities in the Ancient Mediterranean*. London: Routledge.

Fortier, Anne-Marie. 2022. 'The Speaking Citizen: Language Requirements and Linguistic Neoliberal Colonialisms'. *Citizenship Studies* 26 (4–5): 447–453.

Foucault, Michel. 1980. *Power/Knowledge*. Translated by Colin Gordon, Leo Marshall, John Mepham, and Kate Soper. Hemmel Hempstead: Harvester Wheatsheaf.

Foucault, Michel. 1988. 'Technologies of the Self'. In *Technologies of the Self: A Seminar with Michel Foucault*, edited by Luther H. Martin, Huck Gutman, and Patrick H. Hutton, 16–49. Amherst: University of Massachusetts Press.

Foucault, Michel. 1997. *Ethics: Subjectivity and Truth: Essential Works of Foucault, 1954–1984*. New York: The New Press.

Foucault, Michel. (2004) 2007. *Security, Territory, Population: Lectures at the Collège de France 1977–1978*. Translated by Graham Burchell. Basingstoke: Palgrave Macmillan.

Freeden, Michael. 2013. *The Political Theory of Political Thinking: The Anatomy of a Practice*. Oxford: Oxford University Press.

Frost, Tom. 2019. 'The *Dispositif* between Foucault and Agamben'. *Law, Culture and the Humanities* 15 (1): 151–171.

Frug, Gerald E. 1980. 'The City as a Legal Concept'. *Harvard Law Review* 93 (6): 1057–1154.

Gamble, Clive. 2013. *Settling the Earth: The Archaeology of Deep Human History*. Cambridge: Cambridge University Press.

Gerçek, N. İlgi. 2023. 'Citizenship in Hittite Anatolia'. In *Citizenship in Antiquity: Civic Communities in the Ancient Mediterranean*, edited by Jakub Filonik, Christine Plastow, and Rachel Zelnick-Abramovitz, 81–97. London: Routledge.

Gierke, Otto. (1880) 1939. *The Development of Political Theory*. Translated by Bernard Freyd. London: Norton.

Gierke, Otto. (1881) 1900. *Political Theories of the Middle Age*. Translated by Frederic William Maitland. Cambridge: Cambridge University Press.

Gierke, Otto. (1881) 1977. *Associations and Law: The Classical and Early Christian Stages*. Edited and translated by George Heiman. Toronto: University of Toronto Press.

Gierke, Otto. (1889) 1934. *Natural Law and the Theory of Society, 1500–1800*. Translated by Ernest Baker. Cambridge: Cambridge University Press.

Gilio-Whitaker, Dina. 2015. 'Idle No More and Fourth World Social Movements in the New Millennium'. *South Atlantic Quarterly* 114 (4): 866–877.

Golder, Ben. 2015. *Foucault and the Politics of Rights*. Stanford, CA: Stanford University Press.

Gouges, Olympe de. (1791) 2018. *The Declaration of the Rights of Women: The Original Manifesto for Justice, Equality, and Freedom*. Lewes: ILEX.

Hacking, Ian. 2002. *Historical Ontology*. Cambridge, MA: Harvard University Press.

Hacking, Ian. 2007. 'Kinds of People: Moving Targets'. In *Proceedings of the British Academy*, 151: 285–318.

Heater, Derek Benjamin. 1990. *Citizenship: The Civic Ideal in World History, Politics, and Education*. London: Longman Group.

Hindess, Barry. 1998. 'Divide and Rule: The International Character of Modern Citizenship'. *European Journal of Social Theory* 1 (1): 57–70.

Krause, Johannes, and Thomas Trappe. 2022. *A Short History of Humanity: A New History of Old Europe*. Random House.

Kymlicka, Will, and Norman Wayne. 1994. 'Return of the Citizen: A Survey of Recent Work on Citizenship Theory'. *Ethics* 104 (January): 352–381.

Laclau, Ernesto. 2005. *On Populist Reason*. London: Verso.

Laclau, Ernesto. 2007. *Emancipation(s)*. London: Verso.

Latour, Bruno. 2000. 'The Berlin Key or How to Do Words with Things'. In *Matter, Materiality and Modern Culture*, edited by Paul Graves-Brown, 10–21. London: Routledge.

Mann, Michael. 1987. 'Ruling Class Strategies and Citizenship'. *Sociology* 21: 339–354.

Marshall, T. H. (1949) 1996. *Citizenship and Social Class*. London: Pluto Press.

Miki, Yuko. 2018. *Frontiers of Citizenship: A Black and Indigenous History of Postcolonial Brazil*. Afro-Latin America. Cambridge: Cambridge University Press.

Miller, Todd. 2019. *Empire of Borders: The Expansion of the US Border around the World*. London: Verso.

Minahan, James. 2016. *Encyclopedia of Stateless Nations: Ethnic and National Groups Around the World*. 2nd ed. Santa Barbara, California: Greenwood.

Miranda, Luis de. 2013. 'Is A New Life Possible? Deleuze and the Lines'. Translated by Marie-Céline Courilleault. *Deleuze Studies* 7 (1): 106–152.

Moati, Raoul. 2014. *Derrida/Searle: Deconstruction and Ordinary Language*. Translated by Timothy Attanucci. New York: Columbia University Press.

Montesquieu, Charles Secondat. (1748) 1989. *The Spirit of the Laws*. Cambridge: Cambridge University Press.

Mountz, Alison. 2011. 'The Enforcement Archipelago: Detention, Haunting, and Asylum on Islands'. *Political Geography* 30 (3): 118–128.

Nail, Thomas. 2012. *Returning to Revolution: Deleuze, Guattari and Zapatismo*. Edinburgh: Edinburgh University Press.

Nash, Kate. 2010. 'Dangerous Rights: Of Citizens and Humans'. In *Rights in Context: Law and Justice in Late Modern Society*, edited by Reza Banakar, 71–82. Farnham: Ashgate.

Ness, Immanuel, ed. 2009. *The International Encyclopedia of Revolution and Protest: 1500 to the Present*. Malden, MA: Wiley-Blackwell.

Pellegrino, Gianfranco. 2022. 'Politics in the Anthropocene: Non-Human Citizenship and the Grand Domestication'. *Rivista Italiana Di Filosofia Politica*, no. 3: 131–160.

Phillips, Andrew, and J. C. Sharman. 2020. *Outsourcing Empire: How Company-States Made the Modern World*. Princeton: Princeton University Press.

Pocock, J.G.A. 1992. 'The Ideal of Citizenship Since Classical Times'. *Queen's Quarterly* 99 (1): 33–55.

Pownell, Thomas. 1752. *Principles of Polity, Being the Grounds and Reasons of Civil Empire*. London.

Prak, Maarten Roy. 2018. *Citizens Without Nations: Urban Citizenship in Europe and the World, C.1000–1789*. Cambridge: Cambridge University Press.

Prauscello, Lucia. 2014. *Performing Citizenship in Plato's Laws*. Cambridge: Cambridge University Press.

Rancière, Jacques. (1992) 1995. *On the Shores of Politics*. Translated by Liz Heron. London: Verso.

Rancière, Jacques. (1995) 1998. *Disagreement: Politics and Philosophy*. Translated by Julie Rose. Minneapolis, MN: University of Minnesota Press.

Rancière, Jacques. 2004. 'Who Is the Subject of the Rights of Man?' *The South Atlantic Quarterly* 103 (2/3): 297–310.

Riesenberg, Peter. 1992. *Citizenship in the Western Tradition: From Plato to Rousseau*. Chapel Hill: University of North Carolina Press.

Santner, Eric L. 2011. *The Royal Remains: The People's Two Bodies and the Endgames of Sovereignty*. Chicago: University of Chicago Press.

Scott, James C. 1992. *Domination and the Arts of Resistance: Hidden Transcripts*. New Haven, CT: Yale University Press.

Scott, James C. 1998. *Seeing Like a State: How Certain Schemes to Improve the Human Condition Have Failed*. New Haven: Yale University Press.

Scott, James C. 2009. *The Art of Not Being Governed: An Anarchist History of Upland Southeast Asia*. New Haven: Yale University Press.

Scott, James C. 2017. *Against the Grain: A Deep History of the Earliest States*. New Haven: Yale University Press.

Scott, James C. (2017) 2019. *Homo domesticus: une histoire profonde des premiers États*. Translated by Jean-Paul Demoule and Marc Saint-Upéry. Paris: La Découverte.

Sedgwick, Eve Kosofsky. 2003. *Touching Feeling: Affect, Pedagogy, Performativity*. Durham: Duke University Press.

Shaw, Jo. 2020. *The People in Question: Citizens and Constitutions in Uncertain Times*. Bristol: Bristol University Press.

Shindo, Reiko. 2022. 'Decolonising the Language of Citizenship'. *Citizenship Studies* 26 (4–5): 650–660.

Shryock, Andrew and Daniel Lord Smail. 2011. *Deep History: The Architecture of Past and Present*. Berkeley, CA: University of California Press.

Simpson, Audra. 2014. *Mohawk Interruptus: Political Life across the Borders of Settler States*. Durham: Duke University Press.

Sprinker, Michael. 1999. *Ghostly Demarcations: A Symposium on Jacques Derrida's Specters of Marx*. London: Verso.

Tazzioli, Martina. 2020. *The Making of Migration: The Biopolitics of Mobility at Europe's Borders*. London: Sage.

Temin, David Myer. 2023. *Remapping Sovereignty: Decolonization and Self-Determination in North American Indigenous Political Thought*. Chicago: University of Chicago Press.

Tilly, Charles. 1995. 'Citizenship, Identity and Social History'. *International Review of Social History* 40 (Supplement S3): 1–17.

Tilly, Charles. 1997. 'A Primer on Citizenship'. *Theory and Society* 26 (4): 599–602.

Tilly, Charles. 2008. *Contentious Performances.* Cambridge: Cambridge University Press.

Troy, Deirdre. 2019. 'Governing Imperial Citizenship: A Historical Account of Citizenship Revocation'. *Citizenship Studies* 23 (4): 304–319.

Tully, James. 2014. *On Global Citizenship: James Tully in Dialogue.* London: Bloomsbury.

Turner, Bryan S. 1986. *Citizenship and Capitalism: The Debate Over Reformism.* London: Unwin.

Turner, Bryan S. 1990. 'Outline of a Theory of Citizenship'. *Sociology* 24: 189–217.

Vigil, Kiara M. 2015. *Indigenous Intellectuals: Sovereignty, Citizenship, and the American Imagination, 1880–1930.* Cambridge: Cambridge University Press.

Walia, Harsha. 2021. *Border and Rule: Global Migration, Capitalism, and the Rise of Racist Nationalism.* Chicago: Haymarket Books.

Weber, Max. (1921) 1978. *Economy and Society: An Outline of Interpretive Sociology.* Translated by E. Fischoff. Berkeley: University of California Press.

Weber, Max. 1927a. 'Citizenship'. In *General Economic History,* edited by Frank H. Knight, 315–337. London: Transaction Publishers.

Weber, Max. 1927b. *General Economic History.* Translated by Frank H. Knight. New York: The Free Press.

Weibel, Peter. 2015. *Global Activism: Art and Conflict in the 21st Century.* Cambridge, MA: MIT Press.

Wells-Barnett, Ida B. (1893) 2014. 'The Bitter Cry of Black America'. In *The Light of Truth: Writings of an Anti-Lynching Crusader,* edited by Mia Bay and Henry Louis Gates. New York: Penguin.

Wittgenstein, Ludwig. (1953) 2009. *Philosophical Investigations.* Translated by G.E.M. Anscombe and P.M.S. Hacker. 4th ed. Oxford: Blackwell.

Wollstonecraft, Mary. (1792) 2010. *A Vindication of the Rights of Woman.* London: Verso.

Wood, Ellen Meiksins. 1997. *Peasant-Citizen and Slave: The Foundations of Athenian Democracy.* London: Verso.

Wood, Ellen Meiksins. 2008. *Citizens to Lords: A Social History of Western Political Thought From Antiquity to the Late Middle Ages.* London: Verso Books.

Yashar, Deborah J. 2005. *Contesting Citizenship in Latin America: The Rise of Indigenous Movements and the Postliberal Challenge.* Cambridge: Cambridge University Press.

Young, Iris Marion. 1989. 'Polity and Group Difference: A Critique of the Ideal of Universal Citizenship'. *Ethics* 99 (2): 250–274.

Zivi, Karen. 2012. *Making Rights Claims: A Practice of Democratic Citizenship.* Oxford: Oxford University Press.

Index

Note: For table citations, page numbers and number spans appear in **bold**.

For Product Safety Concerns and Information please contact our EU
representative GPSR@taylorandfrancis.com
Taylor & Francis Verlag GmbH, Kaufingerstraße 24, 80331 München, Germany

* 9 7 8 1 0 3 2 4 9 9 0 0 0 *